Y0-BOC-580

Making Moral Decisions

Making Moral Decisions
Living Our Christian Faith

by
Richard Reichert

Saint Mary's Press
Christian Brothers Publications
Winona, Minnesota

Edited by Stephan Nagel

Nihil Obstat: Rev. Benjamin T. Mackin, O. Praem., J.C.D.
                    Censor
Imprimatur: †Most Reverend Aloysius J. Wycislo, D.D.
                    Bishop of Green Bay
                    February 9, 1979

Third Printing—July 1979

Acknowledgments on page 112

ISBN 0-88489-109-7
Library of Congress Catalog Card #79-63483

Copyright 1979 by St. Mary's College Press, Terrace Heights, Winona, Minnesota 55987. No part of this text may be reproduced by any means without written permission of the publisher.

Contents

CHAPTER 1

Moral Growth: Why Should We Be Moral?

1 This Book and You

What you will discover in this book depends a lot on who you are. Generally it tries to help you get a grasp on your life at a time when you might be experiencing confusion and doubts about living morally as a Christian. And while not every case, question, and activity will apply to you as an individual, stick with them because you are likely to find some thought-provoking things here, some life-shaping things, some things that make a lot of sense to you.

Briefly, this book has three purposes: (1) to help you grow as a Christian, (2) to give some of you good news about being moral, and (3) to challenge some of you regarding your moral stance. Each of these purposes deserves some explanation.

To help you grow as a Christian
Many young people your age are facing important decisions: How should I treat other people? Just what am I supposed to do with my sexual feelings and powers? What do I owe the institutions I grew up in — school, church, state, family? What am I going to do after graduation?

While you are certainly practised at making decisions daily, these are some very difficult ones you face. And in making them you may or may not have much advice from helpful sorts of people. Maybe you have broken off diplomatic relations with your parents for the time being, so you can't easily ask their advice. Maybe there just isn't a teacher or pastor or counselor you feel comfortable being frank with. And besides that your friends very likely cannot add much to your own insights. In that case, treat this book as a survival kit for making the tough moral decisions, tiding you over until you feel skillful and find some helpful people to confide in.

To give some of you good news about being moral

Often enough young people look upon their moral future as being pretty dim. Adults in general may seem hypocritical or immoral. Films and TV "heroes" don't offer us much hope or vision because they exist in one-dimensional, unreal worlds brimming over with violence and uncaring relationships. Sometimes it is difficult to see a future in being moral.

The good news this book offers is that you are already a moral person. Everyone shares some moral sense as a part of being human. And besides that you have the great fortune to have been raised in a culture which values the teachings of Jesus. In other words, morality is not something tacked on, which you might easily detach or lose. Rather, it is as much a part of you as your ability to think or to cook or to do gymnastics. And, like these other skills, it improves with practice. But unlike the great athletic heroes or movie stars, the great moral heroes — Jesus, Socrates, Mohammed, Moses, Gandhi — will live on and continue to affect the lives of people almost forever. That's how important and basic morality is to the human race.

To challenge some of you regarding your moral stance

When you were a child, you did things before you understood them. That was fine because children are not expected to act responsibly. For this reason, society does not punish children as criminals, and for the same reason the Church does not call any of their actions sinful.

As you grow up, however, there comes a time when you must begin to be responsible for your actions because (1) your actions are of a more and more serious kind and (2) as Christians we believe that each person has the duty to make moral decisions for himself or herself.

Perhaps you have been using your moral skills for some time now. If so, you may find some of the information in this book is familiar to you. That's fine. On the other hand, if you don't see any need for serious moral decision-making yet, you may have a problem because you will soon face difficult moral decisions without the sharpened skills you will need. In that case, you may have only flimsy or gimmicky answers to fall back on. Or you may find yourself forced to adopt answers from the many people in our society who are all too willing to make decisions for you. Brought to the extreme, certain cult leaders are happy to free their followers from much of their decision-making.

Moreover, it isn't enough merely to accept the attitudes and behavior of those around us. The challenge of Christianity is too great to allow us to do that. As Christians we must always be "movin' on." As Christians we are pilgrims wandering slowly toward a new Kingdom. We spend our lives attempting to make the truth of Jesus and his teachings real. This truth is not something mummified and it is not some burden we carry with us. Rather it is an understanding we bring to the dilemmas we face, and it is a hope with which we confront our misfortunes. In this book we will discuss this Christian perspective more fully.

2 Beginning at the Beginning

Morality begins from the inside, first of all, in the experience of ourselves as somehow unique, somehow different from other animals and things. This experience includes an awareness of what is important to us, what we need precisely because we are persons.

> For example, to be alive, in good health, and free from pain is better than to be dead or in ill health or in pain. Only extreme conditions can drive a person to view death as a better option than life, or pain a better option than comfort.

> As persons we also experience a need to exercise some control over our lives, to be able to make our own choices about what we shall do, where we shall live, with whom we will associate. Whatever robs us of those freedoms we consider evil.

> As persons we want to know the truth and we view ignorance as bad. Whatever prevents us from knowing the truth or from having access to necessary knowledge we consider evil.

> As persons we want to have the assurance that the goods we need for our survival — things like food, shelter, and clothing — won't be taken from us. Whatever robs us of what is rightfully ours is considered evil.

> As persons we feel the need for respect and dignity. We want to be recognized as unique, as worthwhile, as more than a "thing." Whatever robs us of that dignity and respect is considered evil.

> Further, life itself and then freedom, truth, necessary property, and our good name are only *some* of the basic needs we humans experience within us; there are others.

So, whatever we do to injure our own life, to destroy our freedom, to keep us in ignorance, or to tarnish our own dignity we consider as morally bad.

The basis of what we know is good or bad then begins within us, with our self-understanding of what it means to be a human. It extends to others when we begin to recognize others as persons like ourselves and therefore as having the same needs and rights we experience within ourselves. We extend our moral world to include others in relationships of love and faith and justice. We realize, for instance, that lying is bad because it robs the other of the personal right to know the truth. Stealing is bad because it takes from another the goods he or she has a right to precisely because of being a human being. Fighting is bad because it threatens the life and health of another person as well as our own.

Rooting morality in our own experience of human dignity and in the recognition of the dignity of others enables us to identify workable moral guidelines for our behavior. They are not imposed on us from the outside but rise out of our own experience of what it means to be persons and what we need as persons. In working out these guidelines, though, we immediately run into several problems. The first is tribalism, the second is circumstances, and the third is religious experience.

Tribalism

As we just mentioned, our moral codes are built on our self-understanding and on our appreciation of the dignity of others. Where that respect for others fails, we have the phenomenon of *tribalism*. Tribalism means that a certain moral code applies within "the tribe," but not outside it. People outside "the tribe" simply aren't viewed as persons and don't have any moral rights.

For example, the ancient Greeks regarded everyone who was not Greek as subhuman. The word *barbarian* comes from a Greek word meaning anyone non-Greek. The Greeks traced their own ancestry back to the gods and believed that they were created a cut above their neighbors. It was perfectly all right then to rob, lie, cheat, rape, kill, and enslave people of other countries.

Among many primitive peoples only the men had what we might consider person-status. Women were considered inferior, and they were often the personal property of the men. Not being "tribal members," women could be bought, sold, or exchanged like property, and they had no say in the government of the tribe. Because they were the property of a "tribal member," however, it was a crime to have sexual relations with another man's woman.

As narrow-minded as tribalism may seem, it is still very much with us today. In World War II, the Nazis exterminated millions of Jews on the principle that they were subhuman, an inferior race outside the "tribe" called German. Again, not many generations ago the "white tribes" saw nothing wrong in going to Africa, capturing and enslaving the black race, simply because it didn't belong to the same tribe. The racism in our nation today is nothing more than thinly disguised tribalism — the refusal to recognize the personhood of those different from ourselves. Besides black culture, the cultures of Indian and Spanish origin have been ignored or demolished by the failure of "white tribes" to appreciate them or to respect the people who represent them.

As a further example, abortion is legal today in the United States because it has been decided by the courts that the human fetus does not yet belong to the "human tribe" and hence has no rights as a person. In addition, our country is systematically excluding the elderly from "the tribe." Since the old are no longer viewed as members of "the tribe," we are not responsible for what happens to them. They become non-persons.

Bringing the problem closer to the high school situation, most youth would never think of stealing money from a good friend's locker. But since a store owner doesn't belong to "the tribe," some feel it is okay to rip off him or her.

Cliques in most high schools are nothing more than a form of tribalism. The members care for each other and practice a moral code within the clique. But non-members too often are fair game for whatever abuse the clique wants to dish out. Non-members do not have person-status.

Circumstances

We all agree lying is wrong as a general principle. In concrete circumstances do we have a moral obligation to tell a robber where we have hidden our money? Obviously not. As another example, we know in our deepest selves that killing is wrong, but is it wrong to kill to defend your country? your family? yourself? As the circumstances change, we might have to re-think how the principle applies. We can grant as a general principle that every person has a right to the food and shelter necessary for survival. Can we then take goods from another and not consider it stealing? What about our belief that people have a right to their property?

Circumstances make it impossible to apply the same moral norm in the same way all the time. Each moral decision is a unique application of the moral code we experience within ourselves. What we would judge to be morally wrong in one set of circumstances might be good behavior in another.

Religious experience

Let's look at something else that further complicates the process of developing a moral code. It is what we have called the "religious experience."

Once we recognize that we are persons, distinct from other animals, we discover another need within ourselves. We ask, what does it ultimately mean to be human? to be a person? Why do we exist at all? Where did we come from? How did we come to be distinct from other animals? Are we immortal? These are all religious questions, and different peoples at different periods of history have come up with different answers to these religious questions.

These answers alter our understanding of what it means to be a person and hence alter our moral practices. Take, for example, the orthodox Marxist. While a Marxist does not consider the human person immortal — death ends it for the individual — what is immortal is the State. The State is a kind of super-person. Lying and stealing and destroying freedoms are all considered immoral acts by the Marxist. This does not apply to individuals though. Rather, it is wrong to lie or steal or impede the actions of the State. It is okay to do this to individuals if, by doing so, the State is served.

Hinduism, an Eastern religion, believes people are "parts" of the deity, going through a series of lives in the process of being purified from matter so they can ultimately be reunited to the deity. At that time their personal consciousness will finally dis-

appear. Because Hindus see all creation as sacred, they extend the moral principle about respecting human life to include all living things. It becomes morally wrong for them to kill certain animals, for example.

The ancient Romans came to regard one's honor and dignity as one of the keys to the meaning of human existence. To suffer dishonor was the ultimate tragedy. Thus it became a morally good act to kill oneself rather than suffer dishonor, for example, by being captured by the enemy. In our culture it is considered wrong to attempt suicide for any reason.

Another way of looking at religious experience is from the angle of human growth. As children, our religious questions were simple ones: "Am I going to die?" "Is bubble gum good or bad?" "Does God wear hats?" As we grow, we ask the questions differently, seeking more mature answers: "What's going to happen when I die?" "Exactly why did Jesus have to *save* me?" "Can I trust someone to really love me?" The answers our religion provides to these more mature questions affect our moral code and conduct.

So we can say there is a certain commonness found in all cultures regarding moral norms, and all of this commonness is rooted in a common experience of being human persons. We can also see many conflicting moral practices. These are traced to how different peoples have answered the religious questions, the ultimate questions about the origin, meaning, and destiny of the human race. In the next chapter we will discover how Christianity answers these questions.

3 Thinking It Over: Moral Growth

A. It has been suggested that an action is judged good or bad in terms of whether or not it violates the rights and/or dignity that are proper to every person. Check any of the following actions that you would judge as such a violation:

☐ **Lying to one's parents about where you spent the evening**

☐ **Writing an obscenity on a school desk or wall**

☐ **Cheating on a test**

☐ **Smoking pot**

☐ **Reading a pornographic book**

☐ **Sharing a pornographic book with a friend**

☐ **Refusing to report who vandalized the principal's car**

☐ **Getting drunk at a party**

☐ **Skipping Sunday Mass**

Of those you checked, which would you consider the most serious and why?

Of those not checked, why don't you consider it a violation of any person's rights and/or dignity? Be prepared to share and discuss your answers.

B. Imagine how you would feel if you were on the receiving end of the following action:

You are the custodian who has to clean up the mess after the school has been egged or toilet-papered.

Your sister is the victim of rumors about her making it with every boy in town.

You are the store manager who loses his job because his store lost too much money due to shoplifting.

You are the old man on the corner who is ridiculed by a group of kids walking by.

You are the girl who is openly regarded as the ugliest in school.

You are regarded as the most unfair teacher in your school.

Be prepared to share and discuss your feelings.

C. Identify five kinds of tribalism that are most common to your age group, by listing those groups of people who are most typically excluded from your "tribe":

1) _____

2) _____

3) _____

4) _____

5) _____

D. Imagine that *all* forms of tribalism were eliminated within your age group. List five kinds of behavior that would then be regarded as bad (which *in tribes* are considered okay to do):

1) _____

2) _____

3) _____

4) _____

5) _____

CHAPTER 2

Religious Questions: What Do We Believe?

Animals live in two-dimensional time. They can remember a past and can experience a present, but they can't plan for the future. Certain animals instinctively anticipate the immediate future. Squirrels bury nuts and migratory birds move south in the fall, but this really isn't "future think." Rather, it's a reaction triggered by some of nature's influences we don't fully understand. Squirrels don't know why they are burying nuts. It just seems like a good thing to do *today*.

The human animal, namely us, is an exception to this rule. We are three-dimensional. Besides remembering the past and experiencing the present, we can project into the future — make plans, dream, and worry. Because we can think in terms of the future, we can wonder about it, and we can ask questions about it.

It is this "future awareness" that leads the human animal to ask religious questions. Where will I ultimately end up? What am I really to do with my life? Why do I exist in the first place? Who am I? We know we don't have full control over our future, but as humans we naturally wonder who does.

How we answer these questions becomes for us our religion: our value system, our faith, our outlook on life and the world. This religion in turn becomes the framework within which we work out our morality. For example, we mentioned already that Marx answered these questions in terms of the State. He had a fundamental moral code much like ours: it is not good to lie, cheat, steal, or murder. But he applied this code to the State, not to individual persons.

The Godfather (of novel and movie fame) answered these questions in terms of the Family. The Family and its well-being had ultimate meaning for him. He had a moral code which was applied faithfully within the Family. He was loyal to the Family members. He existed to perpetuate and protect the Family and to carry out its "business."

One ancient Greek philosopher, Epicurus, answered these religious questions in terms of pleasure. To experience pleasure was to be fully human. The pursuit of pleasure became a skilled discipline. A badly prepared meal was considered stealing since it robbed persons of a pleasure that was rightfully theirs.

1 Where Do You Get Your Information?

Your personal moral code will have something in common with everyone else's because it arises out of our common experience of being *persons*. But it is still incomplete and basically ineffective for guiding you if your answers to religious questions give inaccurate reflections of what it means to be human.

In fact, because humanity has been asking these religious questions ever since it became conscious that it had a future, it has come up with quite a few conflicting religions.

Some of these religions have been very localized, adopted by a small number of people for a short time — usually due to circumstances. Others have become world religions, dating back for thousands of years. New ones are still being developed today. On the other hand, many persons adopt no religion in its entirety, but pick and choose and develop a very personalized set of religious beliefs.

Also there are lots of people walking around who have not yet asked the religious questions. They are still living on a two-dimensional level, much like other animals. They live only for the present. They take pleasure where they can, and they don't worry about the possible future consequences for themselves or others. They are not yet moral in the strict sense of the word; they don't yet sense that they have any responsibility to the human society. As a result, in some of our cities, people need the courage of pioneers to endure the abuses they must face.

Finally, we must recognize that some people, though aware of their own inner moral code, having had a good education, and having asked the religious questions, nonetheless choose to do whatever they must in order to obtain something they want — money, power, pleasure. They use others, cheat, steal, lie, and even murder knowing full well that what they are doing is contrary to what they know. This suggests that sin is not the outdated concept we sometimes think it is. We will define sin more fully later.

You are perhaps beginning to ask these important religious questions. And probably you have been told since childhood how the Judeo-Christian religious tradition answers them. Now, however, you may not accept these answers with the same unquestioning faith which you probably had as a young child. In fact, such blind, irrational acceptance would be inappropriate for you now. At your age you face the task of "testing out" the answers of Christian tradition against your own growing experience. In a sense that is a life-long task. Moreover, the answers to the religious questions plunge us into mystery. In this sense they will still involve faith. This means whatever answers we arrive at will always be somewhat incomplete, will always leave room for more questing and questioning and thereby finding deeper insights.

More than the answers what concerns us for the moment is the process of questing or questioning. How will we go about seeking answers to the religious questions?

The starting point is our own experience. If our own experience can be used as any measure for finding the truth, however, it will have to meet the following tests. First, it must be *consistent*. For example, do we feel most fulfilled and human when we are with others? in a relationship of mutual friendship? Or do we feel most fulfilled when in isolation from others? in competition with them? when dominating others? One or the other of these two types of relationships must be more human and the other type must be less so. Second, our experience must be *wholistic* — which means it must both make sense to our mind and satisfy our feelings, our gut reactions. For example, a relationship of competition with others or of dominating others may give us a certain sense of emotional satisfaction, but our guts may tell us such a relationship is destructive in the long run. Our common sense tells us that we simply can't take on everyone or try to dominate the whole world. Third, for our experience to be a valid measure of what is true and of what it really means to be human, it must have a *universal application* — it must apply to everyone, not just to ourselves or our "tribe." There is only one humanity so far as we know. Whatever is most deeply fulfilling for ourselves would necessarily be true for all other persons regardless of age, race, or sex. For example, if your experience tells you we humans exist to be in peaceful relationships with each other, you might ask yourself if this holds true for all other persons — even if they have not yet arrived at that conclusion.

Using these criteria to test your experience, you can now ask yourself just what your experience does tell you about several broad categories of concern: relationships, immortality, evil, and happiness.

1) Based on your own experience of being human, what kind of relationship with others seems to you to be most fully human?

2) What are your feelings regarding personal immortality? Do you experience a desire to exist even after death? Do you experience any conviction that you are immortal? On what do you base that conviction if you experience it: a hunch? a feeling? logic? religious faith?

3) What does your experience tell you about evil? Do you feel the world in general and humanity in particular have somehow strayed from being the kinds of realities they are intended to be? Or are we constantly overcoming evil that exists, becoming more fully human? Is there some power that is out to get humanity, something beyond the control of humanity?

4) What does your experience tell you about humanity's chances of gaining or regaining its wholeness if it has strayed from the mark? Do you experience a hopefulness or a hopelessness? What is the source of your hopefulness? of your hopelessness? Is there anything in your experience that leads you to believe there will be a happy ending to human history? to your own history?

5) Based on your experience of being human, what would be a happy ending to human history? What will happiness consist of when humanity has finally arrived at its destiny? Why is there a humanity in the first place?

Some pretty tough questions? You'll want to mull them over for awhile, searching out what your experience can tell you about them up to this point in your life. Keep in mind that you are interested in what you experience as a gut-level response, in what seems valid for everyone, and in what is logically consistent.

2 World Religions

Once you have sorted out your thoughts on some or all of those questions, you will want to measure them against what some of the more durable world religions have come up with in wrestling with those same questions. They reflect hundreds of generations of human experience. We have tried here to identify what all these world religions have in common, rather than talk of the ways they differ. As we have explained, it's the common wisdom, the experiences that seem most universal to humanity, that we are seeking.

World religions and relationships

The common theme of the world religions regarding the relationship that seems most proper to humans is one of some form of unity, of community, of coming together and being together, of communion. Harmony, peace, the overcoming of differences that separate us seem to be marks of this coming together.

World religions and immortality

All significant religions anticipate some form of immortality. It is not seen as *personal* immortality in all of them, however. That is why the whole question of a personal immortality is a pivotal question in comparing the theologies of the world religions.

World religions and evil

All world religions speak of evil having the potential for misleading and even destroying humanity. There is no common agreement as to the origin of this evil, however. Some say evil and its consequent disorder and suffering come from personified spirits or even evil deities out to destroy the work of the good deities (deity). Others see it as an aspect of humans themselves

PANDORA FREEING
THE EVILS OF THE WORLD
by Roberto Magahles
'64-86-22, 1963 (Woodcut)
Philadelphia Museum of Art:
Print Club Permanent Collection

representing the internal struggle between good and evil. Still others see evil as a "not yetness," a temporary state between a chaos prior to creation and the final perfection toward which the whole universe is tending.

On this the religions do agree, however: evil can be conquered or rendered powerless. There is, therefore, some form of salvation for wounded humanity envisioned in all religions. Though the nature and form of that salvation differ widely from one religion to another, all are hopeful and see the possibility for a happy ending to human history.

World religions and happiness

The one common element found in all the religions which describes the happiness for which humanity is destined is the experience of union with the deity who created us. This experience of unity with the deity is the core experience of happiness. The religions differ, however, on how they describe the nature of that union and of the happiness it produces.

This is obviously an oversimplified synthesis of the great religions, but it can serve our purpose here. It demonstrates that there is a certain pattern to how humanity has answered the big questions about the meaning of human existence throughout the centuries.

Humanity is intended to exist in community, unity, communion.

Humanity is intended to continue to exist forever in some manner.

Evil threatens humanity; it can corrupt and destroy.

There is salvation from this evil.

Happiness is related to achieving union with the deity that created humanity.

3 Christianity's Response

The principles outlined in the previous section help in evaluating our own experience of what it means to be human. If we are in strong disagreement with any of them, we need some extremely good arguments to justify our objections to these age-old and universal religious understandings.

These statements of common wisdom don't demand faith in the strict meaning of the word, however. Where faith comes in is in our identifying with one or another of the world religions, saying this one is the best one or the right one. In this matter, we are accepting the word of others and relying on the authenticity of their religious explanations. For example, the followers of Mohammed have never experienced the personal enlightenment or vision that Mohammed experienced. This personal experience of Mohammed is accepted on faith by his followers and is the basis for the Moslem explanation of those truths found in all world religions. The Jewish religion centers on the Exodus experience and on the leader-prophet of that time, Moses. Similarly, Buddhists take the word of the "enlightened one," the Buddha.

Christianity's particular understanding and explanation of those fundamental religious truths is founded on Jesus' understanding of God as his Father and on his resurrection, as reported by his disciples. Because we live in the Christian tradition, we are more concerned with measuring our own experience of being human against that tradition's specific explanation of what it means to be human. We're trying to determine if it gives the best possible guidelines for applying our own inner moral code to the decisions we face in daily life.

Christianity and relationships

Like all world religions, Christianity teaches that human beings are intended to live in unity, harmony, and peace. It is a unity, however, that respects and actually seeks to enhance the uniqueness of each person, that protects the freedom of each person. It is a community that is especially concerned about the weak — those unable to care for themselves, those who need help. The basis for this conviction is Jesus' teaching that each person is specially loved and is precious in the eyes of his Father, the Creator of all humanity. Hence, the fundamental commandment Jesus gives his followers: "Love each other to the same degree that I and the Father love each of you. And remember, we care for you so much we even know how many hairs are on your head."

It particularly should be remembered that because every person ever created is a unique and special object of the Father's love, Jesus is dead set against any form of tribalism. No one is to be excluded from the human community of love. We never have the right to treat anyone as if they weren't human. "There is neither Jew nor Gentile, slave or free, male or female — all are equal in the eyes of God." Any kind of tribalism contradicts what Jesus taught it means to be human. To a large extent his death was a direct result of Jesus' teachings about equality: people didn't like to have such teachings going around; society, as they understood it, would be destroyed. Is this true today?

Christianity and immortality

Central to the Christian experience is the Risen Jesus. From this experience his disciples came to believe in their own personal resurrection. Death is seen as a passage to a new level of life, where even our frail human bodies will reach their full potential of perfection and power. This immortality of both body and spirit accounts for the special respect Christians have for their own bodies and the bodies of other people. The human person is a body-spirit. Human perfection is a body-spirit perfection.

Christianity and evil

While Christian theologians differ when discussing whether there is a personification of evil called Satan, all agree that evil is a reality. It has imbedded itself into the very depths of humanity and has the capacity eternally to prevent individuals from reaching the fulfillment for which they are destined.

Evil is the opposite of love and community. It is hatred of persons, a deliberate alienation from other persons, an entrapment within the self. For the Christian all sin is rooted in selfishness and is destructive of human community.

The definitive act of evil is the attempt to destroy the life of a person: murder. It is the first evil act recorded in the Bible after the Fall of Adam and Eve. Jesus himself was murdered. But Christians believe that it was his act of accepting death that is the basis for our own conviction that evil can be conquered. Jesus' resurrection is proof that evil cannot destroy humanity, even if individuals do give themselves up to evil. Therefore, the basic Christian stance in the face of evil is one of constant hopefulness. We're going to make it!

Christianity and happiness

Happiness, love, and community are inseparable for the Christian. Happiness is to experience loving communion with other persons. Ultimate happiness is the experience of this same loving communion with the Persons of God together with all humanity. Thus, loving community is the highest value for the Christian.

Christian morality is the application of one's inner moral code within this kind of faith vision. For example, every person knows from the inside that good health is better than bad health. So needlessly to harm one's own health or somebody else's has to be bad. But to this universal principle the Christian brings the faith vision that the body is destined for immortal glory. It is even described as a temple, a holy thing. So Christian morality demands more than the usual common sense respect for one's body. It demands a kind of reverence.

To this point we have identified the following principles:

Our own experience of what it means to be a person is the source for our own inner moral code.

Tribalism, circumstance, and religious experience are the chief reasons why there are so many "moralities" even though we all have a certain common inner experience of what it means to be a person.

Answers to the religious questions about the ultimate meaning of human existence are rooted in our own experience but also involve us in what others have experienced — and this involves us in faith.

The Christian's answers to these questions which are described above are rooted in the faith that Jesus is the Risen Lord.

4 The Christian Vision

We wouldn't need to conduct a survey to discover that there are many people who call themselves Christian and profess a Christian faith but who do not act like Christians. We can't let that get in the way of our own evaluation of the Christian faith. In this discussion we aren't concerned with how many people actually live out Christianity. We are concerned with the accuracy of the Christian vision of what it means to be human. Does it make sense? If we followed it, made our moral decisions based on it, would we become more fully human and happy and would the same happen to others? What kinds of qualities would we possess and develop? What would an authentic Christian look like in real life?

Based on Jesus' teachings, particularly the Sermon on the Mount, we can sketch in a broad way how an ideal Christian would approach life and the kinds of qualities he or she would possess:

Ideally the Christian is *hopeful*. That is, the Christian is not overwhelmed in the face of the evil and suffering in this world. While others become cynical, apathetic, or suicidal, the Christian remains positive. With the promise of the Risen Jesus in mind, the Christian hangs in there, continuing to believe in humanity's potential and in all life.

The Christian should be *loving.* Not in the soft, romantic, self-conscious sense where we get the image of a group of people sitting around, holding hands and telling each other how great they are. The Christian — an image of God — is loving in the hardnosed, practical sense of doing love, of being selfless, generous, willing to sacrifice for the good of others.

Ideally the Christian is *prophetic.* Not in the sense of foretelling the future but in the sense of seeing the present for what it really is and then doing something about it. Motivated by the vision of what humanity could and should be in the future — a loving union of all people — the Christian challenges, opposes, tries to overthrow whatever there is *in the present* which prevents us from enjoying community, peace, or justice. The Christian feels responsible for the human condition now!

The Christian should be *creative.* Aware of what humanity is called to be — builders of God's Kingdom here on earth — the Christian actively participates in making it happen. This is the other half of being prophetic or being opposed to oppression and injustice. It is getting involved, stretching one's potential, using one's talent, feeling responsible for creating a future.

HEAD OF CHRIST
by Georges Rouault, French 1871-1958
Oil on canvas
The Cleveland Museum of Art
Gift of Hanna Fund

The Christian should be a *peacemaker.* Not just in the sense of being opposed to violence but in the deeper sense of fostering wholeness, integrity, unity within the self and among all persons. The Christian is opposed to and avoids whatever disintegrates, disrupts, separates us from ourselves, each other, and our God. Violence is the effect of such disunity, not its cause.

The Christian should be a *reconciler.* The Christian can admit to sinning and can recognize it in others. But the Christian also knows that God forgives, and therefore the Christian feels bound to forgive enemies, those who are seeking to do harm. The Christian doesn't just turn the other cheek, but reaches out a hand to restore friendship.

All this may sound too idealistic. If that's what Christians are, no wonder we don't see many of them in real life. That's true, but remember, we said earlier we are growing persons. We are in the process of becoming moral. Morality isn't an abstract set of principles in a book somewhere. Morality is who we are, what we do, what we are becoming. A faith vision like Christianity presents a goal, a direction and demands a commitment from us, a turning to that direction, a *conversion.* Aware of this, we try to make decisions that make us more hopeful, loving, prophetic, creative, peaceful, and forgiving. That's what we are striving to become, not what we already are. As one theologian describes the Christian stance: "We are living in the times between the two comings of Jesus." For that reason, we cannot be entirely satisfied with the present and yet we have everything to hope for in the future.

The above statements are very different from questions like "How much can I steal before it's a sin?" or "How much pot can I smoke before it becomes a sin?" These are nonquestions. They don't go anywhere. They don't look to the future. The only fundamental moral question is this: *Will this action make me and/or others more human or less human?*

For the Christian, being human means being hopeful, loving, creative, and the like. When faced with moral decisions, the Christian asks questions like: Is this a hopeful response? Is this a loving action? Is this going to make me and others more peaceful and whole?

At this point, it isn't a question of whether or not we are Christian. More important is whether or not we continue to ask the religious questions about the meaning of human existence. Our own experience of being human will still remain the starting point, but we should not ignore the experience of hundreds of generations of others as found in common elements of the great world religions. And it would seem logical that we would want to take an especially hard look at the answers our own Christian tradition offers. In any case, we should avoid rejecting that tradition offhand without fully understanding what it is saying or because some Christians don't act very Christian at all.

Looking at it another way, by the time we are sixteen or so, we have already had many years of training and instruction as Christians. Some of it happened in school, but much more of it went on day in and day out at home. Added to that is the fact that we live in a culture which holds Christian values in esteem, even if it often fails to live up to them. So Christianity is part of your mental make-up, and it combines with your needs for life, meaning, dignity, and other human needs to form what we call *conscience*. As we enter into moral decisions or conflicts, it is this faculty, our conscience, which gives the first and deepest response, from our very selves. The next chapters will explain just what moral conflicts are and how we can help to mature our conscience by responding to conflicts honestly and by using special questions to "test reality."

5 Thinking It Over: Religious Questions

A. Think of a time in your life when you experienced the greatest sense of fulfillment as a person. Analyze it using the following guide:

1) **What kind of relationship with other persons — if any — was involved?**

2) **What was your attitude toward time, your sense of time, during the experience?**

3) **What is the biggest obstacle to being able to repeat or continue the experience?**

4) **Can this obstacle ever be removed? How?**

Compare your insights with others and look for similarities.

B. We have identified the following as what the Christian regards as the most important human qualities: hopeful, loving, prophetic, creative, peaceful, and forgiving. Rate each of these in terms of how much you agree or disagree that they are important.

	Strongly Agree	Agree	Not Sure	Disagree	Strongly Disagree
1) Hopeful	☒	☐	☐	☐	☐
2) Loving	☒	☐	☐	☐	☐
3) Prophetic	☐	☒	☐	☐	☐
4) Creative	☐	☒	☐	☐	☐
5) Peaceful	☒	☐	☐	☐	☐
6) Forgiving	☒	☐	☐	☐	☐

C. Using your own experience as the source, develop your own list of the six most important qualities of a fully human person.

1) _Peaceful_   4) _Loving_

2) _Faithful_   5) _Hopeful_

3) _Forgiving_   6) _Creative_

D. Develop similar lists based on what you think each of the following persons might identify as the key elements of being human:

Archie Bunker (comedy character)

1) _Forgiving_   4) _____

2) _Hopeful_   5) _____

3) ~~Is~~ _Family_   6) _____

Kiss (rock group)

1) _____   4) _____

2) _____   5) _____

3) _____   6) _____

Hugh Hefner (publisher of *Playboy* magazine)

1) _Beauty_   4) _____

2) _Sexapeal_   5) _____

3) _____   6) _____

Muhammad Ali (professional boxer)

1) _____   4) _____

2) _____   5) _____

3) _____   6) _____

CHAPTER 3

Moral Conflicts:
What's Important to Me?

Randy has a good chance for a much needed college scholarship if he can "ace" his final chemistry exam and wind up with a higher grade average. Chemistry isn't his best subject, but he has been working hard at it. He hears through the grapevine that someone has come up with the test questions by using a little sleight of hand. Knowing those questions ahead of time would just about clinch his scholarship. Randy's conscience tells him — and he is otherwise convinced — that this kind of thing is dishonest but . . .

That's a moral conflict. What would you do if you were Randy?

Helen is new in school but has been accepted by a group who included her right away. Being shy, she is happy to belong to a group and to make so many friends so quickly. One night everyone is hanging out, bored. Someone suggests that everyone get a can of spray paint and go out and "decorate" the front of a rival school with "appropriate" expressions. This isn't Helen's idea of fun. In fact, apart from the fear of getting into serious trouble, she is convinced such destruction of property is morally wrong. Yet, she doesn't want to put on airs and maybe end up being rejected by the only friends she has in town. The pressure is on . . .

That's a moral conflict. What would you do if you were Helen?

Rebecca's father is a wife beater. For years her family has managed to keep this ugly secret from becoming known. Lately the problem has become more severe — to the point where Rebecca fears for her mother's life. Her mother is without hope and unwilling to help herself. Rebecca wants to seek help, but she is convinced that she would be betraying her family by going to outsiders . . .

That's a moral conflict. What would you do if you were Rebecca?

Judy wants very badly to make the boys' baseball team because at her high school it's the only team that competes at a statewide level. She has had plenty of experience with summer leagues and has fine ability as a pitcher. Mr. Shefner, the coach, tries to coax her out of it by saying that it would make things very difficult for him personally because of the extra arrangements and the criticism it would mean. Mr. Shefner has coached Judy for three summers and has helped her a lot. She doesn't want to hassle him, but . . .

That's a moral conflict. Would would you do if you were Judy?

Carl's seventeen-year-old sister shows promise of becoming a fine musician. She also has been going steady for almost a year, and now she tells Carl she is pregnant. Further, she plans to have an abortion before their parents find out about it. Having the baby, she says, will wreck her chances for a college scholarship in music and for a professional career later, besides ruining her socially now. Carl is convinced that abortion is totally wrong, but he has always been loyal to his sister and proud of her talent . . .

That's a moral conflict. What would you do if you were Carl?

Ben has just been hired to work on a highway construction crew for the summer. The work is hard, but the pay is great at a time when jobs are hard to come by. One day the foreman tells Ben to slow down: "You're working too hard. This crew is used to taking it easy. At this rate you'll put yourself out of a job because once we're done here, you're finished. Work slower — you'll last a lot longer." Ben is convinced that this practice is dishonest to the company and to the taxpayers who are buying the highway work. But he needs the job . . .

That's a moral conflict. What would you do if you were Ben?

1 Moral Conflict — A Definition

From the above examples, which are probably not too far from some real situations you could describe, we can see that every moral conflict has several common elements: (1) We have already formed a rather clear idea of what is morally good or bad in a given situation, of what is the more human thing to do. (2) There is some immediate and much desired good that could be achieved if we act contrary to our conscience. (3) We experience a pull in two different directions.

If we follow our consciences, of course, we will have some inner feeling of peace and wholeness, a sense of having done the right thing. But some undesirable and perhaps far-reaching consequences could follow from a choice based on conscience. For example, if Randy doesn't cheat on the exam, he might miss his chance for the scholarship and maybe even his chance for a college education. If Helen doesn't join the raid on the rival school, she could end up on the fringes of her peer group, lonely and isolated from the friends she so badly needs right now.

Moreover, to be a moral conflict, the judgment of what is right or wrong must be our own, not someone else's. If we don't buy the idea that cheating is being dishonest and thus less human than we could be, we obviously won't feel any conflict in deciding to cheat, especially if an important good can be gained from it. Cheating is a temptation only if we consider cheating as morally wrong. Thus all moral conflicts come primarily from within, from our own convictions regarding right and wrong. Let's take a look in depth at two moral conflicts.

1) You are probably familiar with the story of the rich young man in the gospel. He came to Jesus sincerely seeking to learn what he should do to be saved, that is, perfect his humanness. Jesus told him to keep the commandments contained in the Jewish tradition. The man said honestly that he had been doing that all his life. Then Jesus said, if he really wanted to get serious, he should give all his possessions to the poor and join up with himself and the Apostles. The story concludes with the young man rejecting the invitation and going back home. It adds that "he had many possessions."

2) Rick has met "Ms. Right." Jean is the best thing that ever happened to him. When they are together everything is great. He feels good all over. He begins to like himself for the first time. He is no longer alone. He feels important. He is happy. Rick even improves in his school work. He is more pleasant around the house. He likes people. Life is great. But Rick's parents don't approve of Jean. Even some of his friends advise him to drop her. Jean has a bad track record according to them. She will use him and dump him. Rick wants his parents' and his friends' approval, but nothing they say can convince him they are right about Jean.

Let's take it one step further. The relationship grows to the point where sexual intimacy is the next step. Rick has been taught and has become convinced that pre-marital sex is wrong in any circumstances, but his heart sees it differently. This relationship is an exception. This relationship is so good. Rick feels that whoever said that pre-marital sex is immoral couldn't possibly have experienced the kind of relationship he has right now with Jean.

What is going on here? As we mentioned earlier, we all have certain needs we experience precisely because we are human. For example, all of us need to feel secure, to experience affection, to find meaning, to feel like we are worthwhile. We may or may not be fully aware of these needs, but they keep working anyway. Knowingly or unknowingly we seek to fulfill these needs.

Let's say you experience at this point in your life a strong need for self-worth. If so, you will tend to value whatever gives you a feeling of self-worth. You may try to gain it by success in school, by being popular with your classmates, by excelling in some talent such as music, drama, athletics. To a degree it is a trial-and-error process. But sooner or later certain efforts begin to pay off in satisfying your need to feel worthwhile. And as some effort continues to provide self-worth, you eventually arrive at a conclusion, a kind of unconscious intuition, that this thing — academic success, popularity, excelling in some talent — is *valuable*. It is so valuable, in fact, it should be considered valuable by everyone. If others don't value what you do, it is just because they don't know any better.

What we value, then, can be described as "a personal universal." That means from our point of view this object, quality, person, relationship, or activity is good for everyone, regardless of what others may in fact think just now, and even despite what our own conscience may say about it. This is how a moral conflict happens: something we value goes against what our conscience deems moral.

In the example of the rich young man, he valued his earthly possessions. Why, we can't be sure. Maybe they satisfied a need for security, for prestige, power, or freedom. And he followed the laws of his religion very sincerely. But he wasn't ready to give up his wealth for some unproven path to a higher perfection. While he seems to have known Jesus was right, he valued his wealth and whatever need it fulfilled for him above what his conscience demanded. That was his value conflict.

In the example of Rick and Jean, the relationship clearly satisfies some real need. If parents and friends object, it is only because they don't really understand. They don't really know Jean. They are mistaken. If they did know Jean, they too would value the relationship. And if conscience still objects to sexual intimacy in this instance, then conscience must be mistaken too.

It would be great if what our conscience judges as the moral good and what our heart loves as the good were one and the same. In fact, that is what it means to "have it together." That's what we strive to create in ourselves. When the head and the heart team up together there is no stopping an individual. Great people operate out of that kind of unity.

Everyday experience tells us, however, that we don't often enjoy that kind of unity. Often we experience a deeper kind of moral conflict. This type of conflict is much more involved, more critical than the experience of a one-shot temptation like cheating on an exam. That's a question of experiencing a momentary outside pull, even if it is a strong one. The deeper kinds of moral conflicts affect us at many levels. Decisions regarding sexual relations, for instance, confront the conscience with a whole range of personal needs, growing sexual awareness, demands by others, a rejection of parental values, affirmation of oneself as a sexual person, a certain amount of idealism or romanticism.

What are the options in such a conflict? Frequently we will tend to live with inner turmoil until something happens: (1) because we continue to feel guilty, we decide in favor of our conscience, (2) we settle our conscience on the matter, changing our moral sense about similar decisions in the future, or (3) the situation changes somehow.

2 Needs and Values

Before we take a closer look at what to do on the practical level if we experience this kind of moral conflict, we should know a few more things about what we value in life.

For one thing, while all of us possess the same kinds of needs because we possess a human nature, one or another of our needs may be more important at different times in our lives. Most young children, for example, have a strong need for security. Parental approval usually fulfills this need. They will value approval from their parents more than just about anything else. Whatever gains this approval for the child is what he or she considers morally good. What is bad is whatever causes disapproval.

We all share this need for security. Usually by the time we are in our late teens, however, we have found ways to satisfy it other than just by parental approval. We are secure because of our own talents, because of our experience, because of our friendships. We have an identity that doesn't depend exclusively upon parental approval anymore. What we may need now is greater freedom, autonomy, self-direction. For this reason, we value having a job that gives us some financial independence or having a car that gives us some physical freedom. These might become values for us which take first place over getting good grades in school.

As we said earlier, we aren't always fully aware of our needs. So we aren't fully aware of just why we value some things so much. For example, the person in a relationship with "Mr./Ms. Right" might not be aware that the relationship is really satisfying too great a need for security perhaps. And unless we get in touch with our needs and with just how strong some of our needs may be, we might make wrong decisions based on them. Whatever the need is that an overweight person feeds with the third dessert, for instance, it is obviously a powerful one and it may be the crux of the problem. This issue of needs and their strengths within each one of us can confuse a moral conflict. In seeking the "reality" of the matter, the questions "what?" and "why?" are important ones to ask.

Finally, most of us possess what we can call a *hierarchy* of values. Our stronger needs create stronger values, and our weaker needs create weaker values.

If a need is excessively strong, we will spend a lot of time trying to satisfy it. And excessive needs create disorder in whatever we value. For example, in some cultures males have so great a need to prove their masculinity that it takes first place over things like caring for children and it limits relationships with women to some sort of domination.

In our own culture we have created such an extreme need for material prosperity that we frequently value acquiring money more than preserving nature's beauty and order. Some people are willing to destroy our environment if they can get rich doing it. In sexual matters, women find themselves thought of as "sex objects," to be bid and bargained for.

It follows that our moral decisions are directly affected by how we order our personal values. Slogans like "do your own thing," "if it feels good, do it," or "take care of number one" can be quite revealing of our values — and the kinds of selfish needs out of which we sometimes operate.

This probably is beginning to sound confusing, so a summary might help at this point.

1) All of us have certain human needs that *must* be fulfilled — security, curiosity, meaning, survival, and more.

2) Through experience we discover what we judge as the best, most consistent way to fulfill these needs. What fulfills these needs becomes important to us.

3) What we value as a good based on fulfillment of our needs and what our conscience tells us don't always agree. Hence a moral conflict occurs.

4) We can deal with the conflict by changing our conscience, by rejecting what we value, or by living with the ongoing conflict.

5) Certain needs are stronger at certain points in our life.

6) The stronger the need, the greater we value what fulfills the need.

7) We arrive at a hierarchy of values based on the order of these needs.

8) We can arrive at a disordered set of values because of excessive needs.

Now let's return to the moral conflict between our conscience and something we value.

3 The Difficulties We Face

Resolving a conflict between conscience and something we value involves one of two things. On the one hand there is a serious reexamination of why one's conscience judges a thing right or wrong. This is a rethinking process. It involves one's logic, one's theology, rational arguments pro and con. It demands an open mind and usually involves seeking advice and counsel from others with more experience. In the next chapter we will discuss some important questions which help us to determine what is really going on.

In this rethinking process, we need some very good arguments to overrule our conscience. And it takes time to justify a significant change in that understanding. But it is important to develop an accurate, mature, faith-based understanding of what it means to be human. It is important that our consciences mature fully as we mature.

On the other hand, there is the possibility of rejecting what we value. This usually, but not exclusively, happens because of experience. What we have come to value must be experienced as no longer being the best way to fulfill a particular need. We usually don't change what a person values by using logic, arguments, or rational explanations.

That's why the person in love with "Mr./Ms. Right" will probably never be "talked out of" the relationship by parents or friends. Nor will the person be "talked out of" having sexual intercourse once it is viewed as an integral part of this valued relationship.

The cure — if a cure is in fact needed — will be that the person does come to discover that he or she is in fact being used, or that "Mr./Ms. Right" has many more flaws and weaknesses than first observed, or that sexual intercourse is a "bad trip" outside of marriage. Maybe the other person demands more commitment than we are willing to make. In other words, someone will come to reject the value of a relationship if the relationship itself turns sour, ceases to fulfill the person's need for affection, self-worth, or whatever. As this particular case suggests, it is important to note that relationships either grow or wither. No one can maintain a relationship at just any level of involvement they wish.

This is at least a partial explanation of why so many young people and their parents have problems communicating. Each may be operating out of different needs. And while honest communication helps, arguments don't change values. Only experience leads us to reject something we value.

Parents usually want our happiness and well-being above most other things. Through their own experience they have discovered what *they* consider the best ways to insure this happiness and well-being. So they come up with rules regarding when to get home, where to go, with whom to associate, how much to study, and the like. All the arguments in the world won't change these rules. Behavior conforming to the rules is demanded because it satisfies parents' need to be assured of our safety, our moral well-being, or a successful future.

For your part, you might have the same needs for your happiness, moral well-being, and the like, but you have arrived at different ways to assure those needs are met. You come up with different values — such as certain friendships or a career choice different from the one your parents would choose for you.

Here we see that a moral conflict doesn't always take place within you. It can take place between you and others. Our whole society has been divided at times over such moral conflicts between peoples. The American Civil War is the best example. And it is interesting to note that the United States gradually came around to a more peaceful stance after it had *experienced* the failure of its war policy in Vietnam. Rhetoric usually doesn't change moral values, but experience does.

Closer to home, this means you need to appreciate and to try to understand why others — like your parents — value certain things even if you don't. The beginning of communication happens when both you and your parents understand each other's needs and when you realize how different needs may have different importance.

It's also important that you remain in touch with your needs. You've probably been exposed to value clarification exercises at some point during your education. These can be helpful in gaining an understanding of what you value. They give you a clue about *how* you might act in certain situations, or just *what* you consider important right now. Discovering values is usually done just by observing the kinds of decisions we typically make. If we consistently choose to study rather than watch TV, for instance, academic achievement must be some kind of value for us. Once we discover what we value, however, we must then get at the needs we are trying to fulfill. And then we must determine if what we value is actually the morally best way to fulfill that need.

By way of summary, moral conflicts can take place from within when our conscience and something we value contradict each other. Ideally what we judge as good and what we value as good should be the same, and our moral decisions should flow out of an inner unity. When we don't possess that inner unity, only some kind of change in ourselves can provide it. We must either change the way we think about a particular action or we must reject what we value. Neither kind of change is easy. Either way, decisions like these are turning points in our lives. Finally, there can be moral conflicts between people. If there is to be any kind of communication here and any hope of resolving such conflicts, we must seek to understand what others value and why. Usually this kind of understanding does more to resolve conflicts than do arguments, no matter how logical.

4 Thinking It Over: Moral Conflicts

A. By yourself (or in small groups), develop what you consider a typical moral conflict someone your age could face in everyday life. (Remember, a conflict exists when your conscience says a thing is wrong, but you feel a strong attraction toward it anyway.) Be as concrete and realistic as possible.

Share your moral conflict situation with others in your group or with another group. Then discuss these questions together: Do most people experience these same moral conflicts? Do most people your age judge the particular attraction as morally wrong? Why or why not?

Finally, think up one or more creative alternatives for the conflicts described. Share these with the class and discuss if they are realistic alternatives.

B. Below is a list of some of the more common needs all persons experience because of their common humanity. Circle one or more that you experience strongly and consistently at this point in your life.

1) security	5) respect from others	9) identity
2) freedom	6) affection/friendship	10) happiness
3) meaning to life	7) success	11) equality
4) self-respect	8) inner peace	

Think about how you presently seek to fulfill each need. Write this activity down beside the listed need. Is it working? How important has this activity become for you? Do you think it will always fulfill that need? Would it be a good way for others to fulfill the same need? Now share these valued activities with others in your group to see if everyone would consider them important. Do these activities contradict any of the moral norms you hold or used to hold? Does everyone agree? What is the single most important need for those in your group? Do you agree?

C. Alone or in your small group try to identify what you would consider five basic activities for young people deemed most important by your parent(s) or by most parents. Choose one with which you disagree — one which is not of value to you. Identify what needs of your parents are fulfilled by this activity (look at the list above).

Your Activities	Parents' Needs
1) _____	_____
2) _____	_____
3) _____	_____
4) _____	_____
5) _____	_____

Given these parental needs, are their concerns justified? Is some compromise possible?

D. List five things, activities, or persons you valued very highly as a child that are no longer considered personal values by you.

1) _____

2) _____

3) _____

4) _____

5) _____

Compare your list with others in your group. Any similarities? What does this tell you about your present values? Do you think they again will change significantly when you are 25? 45? Why or why not?

CHAPTER 4

Reality-Seeking Questions: What? Why? How? . . .

A nurse gives a patient a dose of morphine to ease her pain. After work he gives himself a shot of the same drug to get high. For the first act he gets paid. For the second he gets arrested. It's the same drug, same kind of physical act, but different circumstances.

A mother takes a can of spray paint and touches up an old chair. Her daughter takes the same can of paint later and "touches up" some cars in the school parking lot during a basketball game. The mother is being creative. The daughter is being destructive. Same paint, same physical act, but different circumstances.

A person doesn't need to know much about morphine to recognize it is neither good nor bad in itself. And spraying paint from a can is neither good nor bad in itself. What makes some thing or act good or bad are the circumstances surrounding it. That's why even the best, most accurate moral code in the world can only be used as a general guide. It can tell us that it is wrong to kill, but it can never tell us if a particular killing is wrong. We must decide that by considering the important circumstances that surround the situation.

This is not the same as "situation ethics" which denies the existence of any moral absolutes except love. There are many such moral absolutes, and we can discover them from within ourselves. We can say, for example, that killing is immoral, that is, contrary to human instinct and the teachings of Jesus. No one should feel right about killing. In certain cases, however, more than one moral absolute must be considered. Having to kill an airplane hijacker to save the lives of the other passengers, for instance, is a choice between two such moral absolutes, placing the principle of justice above the life of the hijacker. While we continue to assert that killing is wrong, no one should have to carry a guilty conscience from *necessary* forms of killing.

To evaluate the morality of any concrete act before we do it we must evaluate all the circumstances surrounding it. There are a series of questions we can ask to help us here:

What is being done exactly?

Why, with what motive?

How, in what manner, and by what means?

Who is doing it?

When and where is it done?

What are all the foreseeable effects?

Were there any possible alternative actions?

Let's see just what is implied in each of these circumstances surrounding any moral act.

1 What?

When pro-abortion people talk about abortion, they refer to it as terminating a pregnancy. Pregnancy is viewed as a physical state in a particular woman that can be corrected by medical intervention. They focus on helping the woman, concern for the woman's health, protecting the woman's rights.

When anti-abortion people speak of abortion, they refer to it as destroying the life of a living fetus. It involves surgical or other acts intended to stop the heartbeat and other vital signs of the fetus. They are looking at the same operation as the pro-abortionists, but they are focusing on the fetus.

So if you ask one group what is happening in *this* clinic right now, they will tell you a medical cure. If you ask the other group, they will tell you a medical murder. Remember we said that growing morally means we must first of all be honest, willing to confront the reality of a situation. The key is to see a concrete act in its detail and in its entirety to fully understand what is involved, what is really happening or going to happen.

For example, pro-abortion people conveniently refuse to take a good look at what is happening to the fetus in "terminating a pregnancy." They get very upset and shout foul-play when the anti-abortion groups show graphic pictures of well-formed but mutilated fetuses in garbage cans behind hospitals or when they describe processes like crushing the skull of the fetus to stop its heartbeat. Yet that is what "terminating a pregnancy" sometimes involves.

On the other hand, anti-abortionists sometimes refuse to give any consideration to the pregnant woman, her rights precisely because of being a person, her physical, emotional, and mental health. They refuse to admit that there may possibly be instances when saving the fetus involves murdering the mother — emotionally, mentally, or even physically. To decide whether a decision for or against abortion is right, we must know *what* is happening. We must be clear about the fact that a killing — of the fetus or perhaps of the mother — is taking place.

We can use sexual intercourse as another example of how important it is to determine precisely the *what* of an act in order to decide if it is good or bad. Our society is described as sexually permissive. Basically this means many people have come to view sexual intercourse as an act which can be engaged in with the same indifference and casualness as shaking hands — provided it involves two consenting adults. It is seen by many people as a form of recreation or self-expression.

Traditionalists, on the other hand, regard all sexual intercourse outside of wedlock as immoral because they see the act as sacred, a sign of total commitment to another, one of humanity's deepest means of self-giving. It can never be viewed casually or indifferently. Marriage is the proper forum because marriage is a total commitment to another that gives the act of intercourse its true significance. Also, because sexual intercourse is our means for creating new human beings, the stability of the marriage commitment becomes twice as important.

It's obvious that intercourse can be seen in more than one way: it *can* be approached casually — for example, some people do jump in and out of bed with whomever is available at the time; yet it also *can* be a profound act of loving and self-giving, a true sign of a total commitment of body and soul to another human being.

The morality of pre-marital sex, then, depends on *what* in fact is the true nature and meaning of intercourse between two persons. Is it a humanizing act needing the framework of a total mutual commitment between two people? Or is it in fact an indifferent act requiring only that two adults mutually consent to engage in it. (If it is the latter, we can ask why even the most sexually permissive see it as wrong for young children and pre-teenagers.)

Does refraining from sexual intercourse until I have made a total public commitment to another make me more human? In deciding whether sexual intercourse is moral outside marriage, we must understand *what* it is: an act involving all our feelings, thoughts, body, as well as those of the other person. If we are serious about making a responsible moral decision regarding pre-marital intercourse, we must determine *what* it is first.

The same is true about all our moral decisions. We must be very clear on just what it is we are actually about to do, before we can judge it as good or bad.

2 Why?

Motivation — the answer to the question *why?* — is the second important circumstance that determines if a concrete act is good or bad. For example, lying is universally considered bad. But why one lies in a certain set of circumstances will to a large degree determine if that act is bad. Someone might get a false ID card in order to be able to get served in the local bars. Or one might get a false ID card in order to get a much needed job to help support one's family.

In the same way we can do what is universally considered good, but turn it into a bad act by doing the right thing for the wrong reason. For example, someone could devote a lot of time and attention to caring for an elderly aunt. Beautiful! If the sole motive, though, were to get into her will, then a good deed is turned sour by the motive. Again, racing through heavy traffic is a good act when the motive is to get a sick friend to the emergency room. Doing it on a dare makes it a bad act.

Motive is an important question in sexual matters also. Frequently neither person in a teenage couple has much idea of the other person's motives. One psychologist has given this opinion of teenage motives in general: "Boys play at love to get sex; girls play at sex to get love." Do you agree with this statement?

In dealing with motive as part of the circumstances to determine the morality of an act, the real trick is personal honesty. Often we fool ourselves. It's called rationalizing.

For instance, we might con ourselves into thinking that taking the five dollars off Dad's dresser really isn't stealing because he'd probably give it to us anyway. "I just don't have the time right now to go through the hassle he'd put up first."

We might con ourselves into saying we are going to the drive-in because it has the best movie showing right now. In fact, we know there is a pretty good chance for some heavy petting — or whatever.

We might tell ourselves that we are going drinking just for a good time. In fact, we might be trying to obliterate bad feelings about school, family, or ourselves.

Often, of course, our acts involve a mixed bag of motives. We do something partially for one reason and partially for another. We take out the garbage because it's our job — and we want the car tonight. Sometimes we aren't clear on just what our motive is and sometimes our acts are apparently motiveless. It may be an unconscious need that moves us. Remember that it is important to become as aware of our needs as possible.

The more serious the act, the more critical it becomes to sort our motives and to know why we're doing it. The decision whether to have a cola or an un-cola doesn't demand any soul-searching for our motives. The decision to drop out of school requires some pretty good reasons because the rest of one's life would be affected by it.

3 How?

Jake is a high school senior who grew up in a cruel, stern family. Unloved and sometimes beaten as a child, he seeks a cure for his bad feelings by using drugs. In fact, a lot of his hassles do begin to fade — along with his social life and his grades.

Renee's family history was as bad as Jake's. Her father was an alcoholic who could never hold a job. Like Jake, she sought release from the unhappiness she faced daily. She found her achievements as a soccer player relieved somewhat her sense of failure at home — and a college scholarship is becoming a possibility.

No matter how good the action and how noble the motive, the *how* must be taken into account in evaluating a moral decision. In these examples, both Jake and Renee are seeking relief from unhappiness, but Renee's approach offers her options whereas Jake's future is closing in on him. In most instances this is a matter of common sense. Expressions like "two wrongs don't make a right" have been a part of human wisdom for a long time and are usually a good guide in making daily decisions.

But there are some situations where people experience what might be considered a *moral dilemma:* somebody gets hurt no matter how you handle the situation.

Mike's dilemma has to do with who to appoint as the chairperson of the senior prom committee. His friend Al has worked hard all year and wants the position badly. On the other hand, the other class officers — and Mike agrees with them — want Jean appointed in order to improve involvement of blacks in the school which until bussing was all white. What would you do if you were Mike?

Governments face this kind of decision every time they are faced with something like a political hijacking. If they give in to the terrorists and meet their demands, they will be encouraging more such acts in the future. If they refuse and attempt a rescue by force there is a good chance innocent people will be killed.

In these kinds of "damned if you do, damned if you don't" situations, there is no perfect solution. There are, however, two general rules that can help. Both are based on common sense.

The first is: *keep looking for a way out in which no one gets hurt until there is simply no time left and you must act.*

The second is: *choose the method that will cause the least possible harm in the long run.* It's called the principle of minimalism.

We can apply both of these general rules to our example above. Mike might be able to find another job acceptable to his friend Al or to Jean. Or he might consider making them co-chairpersons. If everything else fails, Mike will have to judge between his friendship with Al and the needs of the school at large. Choosing Jean clearly fulfills the wider needs. The hurt to his friend is the minimal hurt.

Fortunately, we seldom face life and death kinds of dilemmas in our daily lives. But there are some. A friend might be heavily into drugs and now pushing to support his habit. How do you help? To turn him in might mean a cure, but it might also mean a jail term. Not to turn him in might mean continued freedom (and the freedom to continue pushing drugs) but early death. That's a dilemma.

A pregnant teenager doesn't believe in abortion but neither does she want to "kill" her parents through the grief and shame they would experience if she went public and carried the baby to term. That's a dilemma we'll come back to a little later.

4 Who?

A little girl goes into a drugstore, picks out her favorite comic book, and walks out without paying. The manager catches up to her and gives her a good lecture. A sixteen-year-old tries the same stunt with her favorite magazine, and she winds up facing criminal charges.

A mentally retarded adult suddenly begins taking off all his clothes on a busy street. The police escort him back home. The local banker does the same thing; he is arrested for indecent exposure.

In these cases we see that *who* is an important circumstance in evaluating the good or bad of concrete actions.

When the *who* is *you,* several principles are involved. For instance, the fact that "everybody does it" doesn't automatically make it okay for *you*. The fact that "nobody does it" doesn't automatically mean it would be wrong for *you* to do it. The majority opinion can never automatically determine the morality of concrete actions involving *you*. You have to decide if the concrete act will make *you* more or less human, regardless of how good or bad it is regarded by the majority.

Just because most people your age can drink six cans of beer and not have bad effects doesn't mean you have the same capacity. You have to determine that for yourself, based on your own physical make-up.

For most other people, to eat six eggs and a pound of bacon for breakfast would probably be an act bordering on ridiculous — and dangerous to their health. It might be a normal act for you at this point in your life. So who you are makes a real difference in the concrete. Again, while TV and film heroes find sexual relationships quickly and painlessly, for us real people things are not often so simple and smooth.

The person you are is more than physical, of course. Your education to this point, your religious convictions, your upbringing are also part of you. So are your talents and other assets. So are your limitations, physical and mental. All that is part of the *who* circumstance when you make your moral decisions. And *who* you are changes as you grow and mature. With these changes, your decisions will also mature. For example, if you have had the opportunity to have a good course on the nature and harmful effects of the various drugs going around, it would be a more serious act for you to go ahead and experiment than it would if you never had this information.

The *who* is very important if we must evaluate the actions of others. For an authentic conscientious objector, to evade the draft could be an act of bravery. For someone else, the same act could be one of cowardice.

The rich coed seeking an abortion is not the same person as the mother of eight who is living in the worst kind of conditions. A wrong becomes more wrong depending on who does it.

The rich man gives a thousand dollars, the poor widower gives five. Who was the more generous? A good becomes more good depending on who does it.

The *who,* then, helps determine not only if a concrete act is good or bad, but also helps determine just how good or how bad two seemingly identical acts are.

Finally, the *who* circumstance includes the other persons involved in our decision. In a negative sense we can see this easily. Stealing is bad. But it is worse to steal somebody's last dollar than it is to steal a dollar from an oil tycoon.

In a positive sense a good act can become a better one depending on who is the recipient. To help someone out of a jam even though she has been spreading all kinds of lies about us is a more noble act than to do the same thing for a good friend. Why do you think that is so?

THE COURAGE OF FULL VISION
by Mirtala Bentov
Bronze
Courtesy, Pucker/Safrai Gallery
Boston

5 When and Where?

In talking about the legal limits to our right of free speech, somebody will always come up with the example that we have no right to yell "Fire" in a crowded movie house. Recently a popular comedian posed a new moral problem: can we yell "Movie" in a crowded firehouse?

Without answering that question we can say that *when* and *where* we do things can significantly alter their morality. Hunting squirrels is an acceptable sport. Hunting squirrels in the city park isn't. Driving fast is fine at the racetrack. It is wrong in a school zone at three o'clock.

Burning trash is necessary. Setting fire to the trashcan in the school lavatory isn't.

We don't have to be moral theologians to see the differences. Our common sense is sufficient in deciding whether the *when* and *where* are important considerations in moral decision-making.

6 Consequences?

"Don't do the crime if you can't do the time." The phrase from the theme song for the Baretta TV show is one way of expressing what we mean by *consequences* as a moral circumstance. We must be willing to accept responsibility for the consequences of our moral decisions — *all the consequences we can reasonably foresee.*

The key here is "reasonably foresee." Every year or so we read in the newspaper where some college freshman died as the result of a fraternity initiation. Sometimes the "hazing" was clearly dangerous, and those involved are considered directly responsible for the death. In other instances it turns out that the student had a heart ailment or some other problem no one knew about. The hazing wasn't risky in itself; it was just too much for that person. Those involved may feel a lot of guilt, but they aren't judged criminals. In many forms of law, however, "ignorance is no excuse." As often as not, then, we must accept responsibility for *any* consequences of our acts, whether they are foreseen or not. Of all the circumstances surrounding our moral decisions, then, this one — consequences — perhaps demands our most serious attention. Too many of us suffer from what might be called moral shortsightedness. We don't look beyond the immediate good we have in mind to the bad side effects. Nor do we see these results in terms of the concrete, personal suffering we might cause.

Recently there has been a TV ad pointing this out. It's the one where a couple of kids "liberate" a stop sign so they can put it in their room. With the sign gone, the ad ends with the sound of screeching brakes and a sickening crash. It makes its point well.

What might seem like a little mischief a group gets into to relieve boredom can have some terrible long-term effects — many of them foreseeable if only we stopped to think.

A group of kids decides to smash some rural mailboxes just for kicks. Hardly the crime of the century, true. But those mailboxes belong to *persons,* maybe elderly persons who can ill-afford the cost of buying a new one much less the aggravation of going to buy it and installing it. What seems like a prank can take on a very serious moral dimension when you translate it into real effects on actual persons.

Shoplifting is another case in which long-range consequences come into play. Usually what people take, especially young people, is "nickel-and-dime" stuff: a record, a blouse, some gloves. Certainly it won't put a big store out of business. And the reason it won't is simply because the store raises its prices to cover its losses. Everybody ends up suffering in the long run. Those who end up suffering the most are those who are already suffering enough, namely the poor who can't handle the rising costs.

The decision to smoke marijuana is another good example of consequences playing a crucial role. The immediate consequences seem harmless enough: a mild high with no hangover and no addiction involved. If it's both legally and morally acceptable to drink liquor with moderation, it should be just as legal and just as morally acceptable to smoke marijuana with moderation. The problem is we simply don't know the long-range effects of marijuana on the human body. There have been many studies but most of them conflict with each other. Some have linked marijuana, even when used moderately, with permanent brain damage, with genetic deformation, and consequently with birth defects.

Such studies are disputed, of course, and other researchers claim there is no evidence that marijuana causes any permanent damage either to the brain or one's genetic system.

What does one do here? We simply don't know what it means to smoke marijuana; we don't really know what the consequences may be but there is some evidence that it may do serious harm.

These are called risk situations. We have to ask some new questions before we can make a moral decision here. (1) Can we justify the risk? In other words, what is our motive for wanting to take the risk? (2) How important is the immediate good we seek? (3) Can we avoid the risk without harming ourselves or anyone else? (4) Can we wait until we can get all the facts?

In many ways it is unfair to equate smoking marijuana with playing Russian roulette, but there is one similarity: smoking marijuana is also a risky game, often an attempt to kill boredom. So it's hard to justify taking the risk of ruining ourselves in the long haul until we can be sure the drug really is safe. Here we see that more than one reality-seeking question can apply to any situation. *Why* we take marijuana is as important as the *consequences*. This holds for any drug: if we use drugs to cover up real problems or to bolster a failing sense of self-respect, then the motive becomes important to our decisions about continuing to use drugs.

One important thing about *consequences* is that there is no such thing as a totally private moral act with totally personal consequences. Whatever a person does affects others at least in so far as it has an effect on his or her relationship to others.

Two young people may decide that they can justify pre-marital sex on the grounds that they are truly in love and do plan to marry in the future. They keep their relationship secret, of course, because they don't want to get their parents upset.

In fact, a consequence of their decision is an altered relationship with parents and others. Most probably they will find themselves having to lie about where they have been, having to sneak around to get birth control devices without being discovered; they find themselves being less open with friends. Becoming cut off from friends and family is a consequence of their decision, and it affects many others, and it must be included in any moral evaluation of their decision.

7 Options?

In an earlier section we described a pregnant girl who didn't want to have an abortion but didn't want to hurt her parents either. She seems trapped in a "no win" situation, a moral dilemma.

It often happens though that what seems like a dilemma really isn't. There may be alternatives we just haven't thought about which would enable us to act in such a way that no one really gets hurt.

In the case of the pregnant girl, for example, it might be possible for her to go live with relatives until after the baby is born. Marrying the father is a possibility, but it is seldom to be recommended. She may be overestimating the hurt she would cause her parents. Maybe they are capable of being much more understanding and much less affected by what others might think than she realizes.

We could challenge a decision to abort on several other grounds, too. Temporary hurt feelings and the pain of embarrassment must be weighed against the much greater evil of killing a human fetus.

But our point here is that when making moral decisions which involve a mixture of some good and some bad outcomes, we have to check out all possible alternatives first. We have to be creative. Too often people end up making bad moral decisions not because they are bad people. They are just uncreative; they give up too easily; they don't think through their *options;* they fail to seek advice.

What seems like a unique moral dilemma to us, one we can't possibly seem to escape, might in fact be a rather common problem with a rather simple solution. Imagine a boy who feels more and more guilty about what he steals from his parents. He is beginning to see himself as a thief. By luck, a friend puts him onto a job which allows him to earn his own money. What looked like a life of crime suddenly becomes trivial in his eyes.

8 The Real World

At first glance it would seem that if we must check out all the circumstances before we make a moral decision, we'd never get around to making any. By the time we checked everything out, one or another of the circumstances might change. And it would probably be a month later.

In practice, of course, such a thorough and detailed checking out is usually required only when you are making significant decisions that have a serious impact on your life and those of others.

Moreover, it is rather rare for what are generally considered bad actions — like stealing, lying, doing physical harm to another — to be turned into good moral actions because of circumstances. They usually involve extraordinary situations like extreme poverty, extreme danger, an extreme emergency. Sure, it may be necessary to kill in self-defense, but how many times a week does that situation come up in your present life? It may become necessary to steal to get money to feed your starving family, but chances are you don't have to struggle with that kind of decision — and never will.

Often it is enough to check out just two or three of the key circumstances to make a moral choice. What is being done? Why am I doing it? Who is involved? What are all the foreseeable consequences, both short and long range?

To this point we've seen that most of us can discover within ourselves an inner moral code, an awareness of how we want to be treated precisely because we are persons. This personal code is refined, given more exact meaning, through our religious convictions regarding the ultimate meaning and purpose of human existence. For example, one's inner moral code dictates that murder is wrong. The Church teaches that abortion is murder. Agreeing with the Church's teaching, we would define abortion as morally wrong.

This interaction between our inner moral code and its religious refinement — our conscience — becomes our starting point in making moral decisions. Using this moral sense of ours, we know in a general way that something is either good or bad. The final test, though, is the circumstances that surround the act. As we have clearly seen, circumstances can make a normally good act bad and a normally bad act good. The reality-seeking questions help define the problem.

9 Thinking It Over: Reality-Seeking Questions

A. Take a few minutes to read Matthew's gospel, chapters 5-7. Do you think that following Jesus' instruction would make you more human? Why? Does that kind of teaching have any *practical value* in terms of the decisions you face? Are there any particulars that you can't agree with? Which ones? Why?

B. Think through the last significant moral decision you made that you considered a morally good one. Jot down a key word or two that would describe each of the circumstances surrounding it:

1) What? _____ 4) Who? _____

2) Why? _____ 5) When and where? _____

3) How? _____ 6) Consequences? _____

What do you think were the key circumstances in determining the decision?

What changes in circumstance could have made this good decision become a morally bad one?

C. As a group, choose one of the moral conflicts which begin chapter 3. Together analyze it: Is it an authentic or presumed dilemma? Can anyone think of alternatives that could resolve the problem in a way that no one gets hurt? Which course of action does the least harm to the most people?

D. We have described the marijuana question as a moral problem. What are your feelings about it? What kind of advice might you give to a younger brother or sister who has access to it?

E. Think of a specific store in your area. Think of an item worth about $5.00 in that store. Suppose you are thinking about lifting it. You know it isn't right, but it surely isn't a horrible crime.

Now list as concretely as possible all the foreseeable consequences of the act in two columns: good and bad consequences. Be sure you identify all the *persons* this affects or could possibly affect. Do these consequences turn the act from "slightly wrong" to rather seriously wrong? Why or why not?

MARTIN LUTHER KING
by Ben Shahn and Stefan Martin
'66-101-4, 1966 (Wood engraving)
Philadelphia Museum of Art:
Given by Mr. Albert J. Caplan

CHAPTER 5

Moral Lifestyles:
How Do We Grow Morally?

1 Negative Patterns in Our Decision-Making

There is a scene in the movie, *The Godfather,* where the son, who had to this point stayed out of any direct involvement in the family "business," makes the decision to avenge the attempt on his father's life. His whole life takes on a radical new direction at that moment. He becomes committed to a life of crime and violence.

The decision to attempt to burglarize the Democratic headquarters in the Watergate was just one rather minor decision. But it reflected and initiated a whole pattern of deceit and underhanded dealing. That's the reason it had consequences far greater than the crime itself seemed to warrant.

Peter, in a moment of panic, denied that he ever knew Jesus. He even repeated the denial several times. Minutes afterwards, though, he regretted that decision. Judas decided to report to the temple police where they could find Jesus. Like Peter he betrayed his leader. Just how were these decisions different?

In these four examples we can see several different kinds of moral decisions. The first example is the kind most people make only a few times in their lives, usually at key moments or when they reach a kind of moral crossroads — which way do I go on? It seldom happens that we take our whole life in our hands and give it a totally new direction by making just one decision.

More typically our life is made up of little decisions that begin to set a pattern. The decision to use illegal means to try to win a political campaign, as in the decision to burglarize, was just one of an apparently long string of little decisions to be less than honest and less than legal. In itself, the one decision could be judged as a kind of petty crime. But seen against a whole background of illegal actions, it became the last straw that forced a president to resign and sent many public officials to prison.

Some of our moral decisions are made in haste, under pressure, in a moment of fear, passion, or anger. We remain responsible for them and their effects. In normal circumstances we wouldn't make the same kind of decision. It goes against our pattern, and we change our mind when things return to normal. Peter didn't make a habit of rejecting Jesus. Just the opposite. So we see him return to loyalty once he regained control of himself. In other words he reverted to form, to the pattern of loyalty he had built up over several years of following Jesus.

Judas, on the other hand, seems to have acted out of a different pattern when he betrayed Jesus. The final act seems to have been the last in a long line of growing doubts about Jesus and his claims as the Messiah. It was a decision arrived at calmly and logically if not joyfully. The gospel suggests a pattern of betrayals by Judas, such as his stealing out of the common purse.

We're getting at something obvious. Moral decisions have different overall effects on our growth in humanness. A few times in our life we may make conscious decisions which definitely change the direction of our lives. We firmly plant ourselves on a new path. Such might be the decision to leave the Church, to get a divorce, to publicly declare oneself gay, to resign from a job, to leave school.

Such decisions, of course, don't come out of nowhere. They usually reflect a pattern that has been building up. They are unusual in the sense that we fully *know* what we are doing. We are consciously choosing to give permanence to a direction that has been building up. In *The Godfather* the son associated with murderers and did not disapprove of their actions. That's the background for his conscious decision to become a murderer himself. More often we make little decisions. Taken together they gradually become a pattern. Most people don't get up one morning and decide *to become* cheaters, liars, or thieves. They get up one morning and — to their surprise — discover that they *have become* cheaters, liars, or thieves.

That's why, in terms of our own moral development, we should usually be as concerned with the pattern of our moral decisions as with any individual decision.

To cheat on an exam may not be a big deal in itself. But it can be one more step toward *becoming* a *cheater-person.* Telling lies to your parents, your teachers, or your friends isn't some grave moral depravity by itself. If the pattern continues, however, one *can become* a *liar-person.*

Maybe slipping a few dollars out of the cash register where you work isn't grounds for life imprisonment. In time, however, many such moral decisions can *turn us into thief-persons.*

2 The Will to Good

It follows that making good moral decisions can become just as much a habit as making bad ones. One psychologist describes this as our "will to good." Each time we decide to tell the truth when faced with an impulse to lie, we *are becoming honest persons.* Observe the continued stress on the word "become." Being moral is *a process* of developing our conscience. Moreover, we must also learn to choose the more human. Through our choices we are becoming. We are literally "creating" ourselves.

That's why, contrary to popular opinion, Christian morality is essentially positive, not negative. Christianity is a challenge to become more perfect, rather than merely to avoid certain sins. Christianity is a challenge to become fully human rather than merely to not break laws. Christianity sets forth an ideal to strive for rather than merely pointing out temptations to be avoided. It is a call to living fully rather than just avoiding illness.

There's no question that many people regard Christian morality as a negative code of commandments and laws, a restrictive list of do's and don'ts. If they are followed, you won't go to hell. In fact, that is how many Christian adults were taught as children.

Such a list of laws and commandments has a place, of course. Laws describe the minimum one must do (or avoid). Such a minimum is like the label on a breakfast cereal box which lists the minimum daily requirements. There's no guarantee you'll reach physical adulthood by eating the minimum vitamins. At best you'll be kept alive.

Doing the minimum might keep a person from gross immorality, but it is hardly enough to guarantee one will become a moral adult. It is similar to studying enough to get a passing grade but not enough to get an education. It has been said that law is found at the foot of the mountain, and that once we break the law and leave the mountain, we are headed for the pit. Christians, however, see themselves as called to the top of the mountain instead of seeing how close they can come to the pit without falling into it.

When it comes to making moral decisions, it isn't enough to decide which is the *good* action and which is the *bad* action. It means trying to discover what is the *best* action. In Christian terms, the best action is one which helps us become more loving, hopeful, helpful — all the traits which we described in an earlier chapter as aspects of Jesus' vision.

Let's use a simple example employing this perspective. If some boy takes advantage of a girl, seduces her, manipulates her emotions to the point where he can use her for his own pleasure, most people would consider that a bad act or a dirty trick. Can you then consider yourself good if you've never used another person in such a way? Not much because that's the minimum. We don't congratulate ourselves each day we don't beat somebody up.

We can congratulate ourselves, though, when we go out of our way to help others grow in self-respect, gain a real sense of self-worth, or overcome self-hatred. We do it by the way we speak to them, treat them, relate to them, respect both their person and their body.

Someone snatches the purse from some poor defenseless old lady. We all agree it is a terrible and cowardly thing. But we don't have a right to be proud if we haven't been purse snatching — or if we only snatch purses from strong, rich, young women. We do deserve some degree of praise though when we go out of our way to make life more pleasant for poor, elderly, and defenseless people.

Not gossiping or not putting people down is okay, but it is minimal. Defending someone's reputation against such gossip or confronting the local putdown artists is better.

All this relates to the message Jesus was trying to get across when he told his followers things like: It's not enough just to be good to your friends. All people in their right mind do this. You should be good to your enemies, forgive them, turn the other cheek, walk the extra mile, give not only your coat but your shirt.

It was from within this faith stance that St. Paul declared that "a man is not justified by works of the law but through faith in Jesus Christ." The minimum may *keep* us human but Jesus called his followers to *become fully human* — to learn to love so strongly that we can conquer, can rise above even the hatred and meanness of our enemies. To be human means to be able to love. To be fully human means to exclude no person from your love — to be able to love that powerfully. That was — and is — Jesus' challenge. As we mentioned earlier, Christians live in this dynamic situation: pushed out of their past and pulled toward the coming Kingdom of God.

To be authentically human and moral, then, means more than making decisions to avoid what you judge to be immoral actions. It means making decisions to love and to transcend self. Until that can be grasped and appreciated, Christian morality doesn't make much sense: it will still be regarded as a joyless set of restrictions on our behavior.

So being moral must be viewed as more than avoiding the inhuman. It means seeking to discover and do the more human. As in all other kinds of moral decisions, the decision to do "the more human" thing must be reviewed in the light of all the circumstances affecting it. As said before, morality never exists in a vacuum, in the abstract. A good example is presented in the popular slogan: "If you give a person a fish, he has food for a day. If you teach him to fish, he has food for a lifetime." Giving to the poor is usually a human and good act. But helping them to help themselves might be the more loving act. What you do depends on the circumstances, such as how badly they need food today.

Also, as with other kinds of moral decisions, in determining what is the more human thing we can experience conflicts, problems, and dilemmas.

Tom knows he should take time to write or visit his grandmother. But he feels an immediate pull to watch a TV special instead. That's a kind of moral conflict. Obviously, watching TV, even in this instance, isn't immoral. We don't usually become less human by watching TV. We just don't grow to the fuller humanness we would have if we did the more loving thing.

Karen may really want to do what she can to help victims of racial prejudice. But it is not clear to her if she should support or oppose bussing in the process. She doesn't have enough information. That's a kind of moral problem.

Chad wants to help minorities get their share of good jobs or their share of positions in places like medical schools. In doing so he might be putting other deserving non-minority people out of work or keeping them from medical school. That's a kind of moral dilemma.

3 Moral Heroes

What can all this mean on the practical level? Let's suppose we have come to interpret our own inner moral code of being human pretty much in the light of what Jesus has done and taught us. Let's suppose that we have gotten into a pattern of following this conscience we have developed.

We typically tell the truth, respect other people's property and their reputations.

We respect and care for our own body. We don't use others for our own pleasure, and so forth.

We have our share of moral conflicts where we're pulled by an immediate good to act contrary to what we know is right. Sometimes we give in, but not often enough to consider that we've developed any pattern.

We may lie once in a while but we haven't become a liar-person.

We may play around with sexual fantasies, but we haven't become a sex-obsessed person. We're still in control of ourself.

We may have gotten drunk a couple times, but we aren't drunks.

If this is the case, we probably feel rather good about ourselves. We feel pretty well put together. We are maintaining our humanness despite all the attractions to do the less human thing.

Can anyone really expect us to do more? Isn't it pretty much a full-time job just to hang on, to resist society's pressure to take pleasure where we can, to take care of number one, and to use others to get what we want?

Aren't ideals like turning the other cheek, sacrificing self for others, or going the extra mile just that — "ideals"? Sure, once in a while we might be expected to rise to the occasion, to do a really noble or heroic thing. But to make a habit of it, to develop a pattern or moral lifestyle of heroism — isn't that a bit too much?

If we approach it literally as a black or white issue, it does sound a little unreal. Nobody says "I am going to do heroic things today," while brushing his/her teeth.

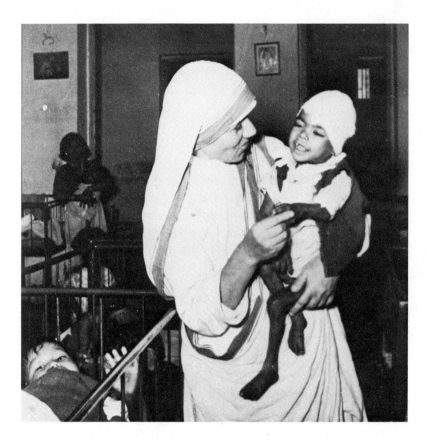

What we're talking about is a direction, a pattern in our choices in the little, everyday situations we face. We see we become liars by developing a pattern of lying. In the same way we become hoping, loving, creative, prophetic, peaceful, and forgiving persons by creating a pattern of choosing the more hopeful, loving, prophetic, or forgiving thing in the daily situations we face.

The present lifestyle of a person like Mother Teresa of Calcutta is truly heroic by any standard. She is dedicating her whole life and every ounce of her strength to caring for the most destitute people in the world. But she didn't get that way overnight. It developed out of a lifetime of decisions to be more generous, concerned, and self-sacrificing in many hundreds of situations. She grew in her ability to accept ever greater challenges to the point that — even unknown and unplanned by her — she has acquired a heroic ability to love.

To put it into another framework, becoming a moral hero is a lot like learning feats of magic, as Doug Hennings once described the process in an interview. He said first he practices a magic trick until it is a habit. Then he continues to practice it until it becomes quite easy for him to do. Even then, he practices some more until finally the trick is so simple for him that it becomes magical for people watching it.

So it isn't a question of making a decision to be heroic and then being heroic all the time. It's deciding on a direction, a set of moral values. Some people aren't ready for this kind of commitment to the "more." They are still having trouble doing the minimum. They aren't even sure if all the minimum, like refraining from pre-marital sex, is all that necessary. They can't yet see anything wrong with it, or with a little cheating or a little lying, or with a little gossip or a little putdown. It is still enough for them to avoid murder, armed robbery, and rape.

People like that still have a lot of things to work out. They are still operating out of a rather primitive or immature morality. But once people become comfortable with the minimum (for our purposes, let's consider it the minimum described in Christianity) and have formed a pattern of at least doing the minimum, it seems logical to suggest that they now continue their growth rather than fall backward to maintenance of the minimum.

It's a question of focus. If you regularly ask how you could make your parents, your friends, your classmates more happy today, it's surprising how seldom you'll find yourself wanting to use others for your own purposes. In other words, the minimum takes care of itself once you focus on the "more."

But even asking that kind of question regularly — "What can I do for others today in this situation?" — seems too idealistic. How many people actually live that way on a regular basis? Not enough, obviously. But actually many more than you might imagine. You don't notice them. They are doing little things, little kindnesses, little acts of concern like taking time to talk to the kid who is down, or being nice to the old man who has to walk past the school yard each day. Next time you step into a car — or better a plane — think of how many people cared enough to build and maintain a vehicle we can use safely.

As with any other challenge presented to you, you are free to accept moral growth or to reject it. No one has a right to force you to be more good than good. No one can force you to be a courteous driver; society can only demand that you obey the traffic laws. Your parents can expect you not to steal from them, but they can't demand that you go out of your way to please them. Only you can ultimately decide how to apply your conscience and your honest appraisal of the situation, and only you can decide if you will follow that decision. Only you can decide to accept the challenge to continued moral growth or to reject it.

4 Thinking It Over: Moral Lifestyles

A. In each of the statements below, underline the activity which better describes how you usually respond, based on your past choices:

1) Go to a play or try out for a play

2) Put off your homework or get it out of the way as soon as you can

3) Arrive early for an appointment with a friend or arrive late for an appointment with a friend

4) Try to get revenge when a person puts you down or laugh it off

5) Seek advice when facing a problem or try to work it out alone

6) Argue with your parents or try to see their point of view

7) Use some free time just to be alone or seek out friends when you have free time

8) Lie under pressure or tell the truth even when it hurts

9) Look for chances to get some exercise or look for chances to get some extra TV time

10) Put down people whom you don't like or try to be nice to everybody

You don't have to share this list with anyone. Just examine it and decide if you can see any patterns developing that you don't particularly like. Any you do like? Any that are actually beginning to shape you as a person?

B. Can you think of any personal decisions you have made in the last two years that have given your life a radical new direction? If yes, did the decision(s) sneak up on you as a result of a trend or did it come upon you suddenly? Would it be hard or easy to reverse that decision now? Would you want to? Why or why not?

THE QUIET MAN

CHAPTER 6
Sin:
What Can We Do About It?

1 Sin and Relationships

There was a magazine ad a while back with a picture of an apartment door loaded with five or six locks and anti-burglar devices. Its message went something like this: "People weren't meant to live this way." (The ad promoted burglar alarms.) The idea behind the ad is that people shouldn't have to live in fear, protecting themselves from others behind locked doors. Without intending it, that ad makes about the best statement one could make about the nature and effects of sin.

For some time the topic of sin has not been popular. Many people have come to consider it an outdated concept from another era. All the idea of sin did, they felt, was produce unnecessary guilt and psychological hang-ups. Unfortunately sin is a reality. No discussion of morality is complete without confronting it. Part of growing up is becoming responsible for the harm we do and finding ways to heal the hurt and sickness that harm creates. Helping us to do so is the purpose of this chapter.

If we look closely at those things we have identified as human traits — truthfulness, respect for one's body, respect for the rights of others — we will see that they all have one thing in common. They are all ways of relating. Being human means being in relationship — with others, with self, with all God's creation, with God.

If we look closer yet, we will see that being human means being in a special kind of relationship. It is a relationship best described as love. Being human means loving. Being moral means loving. Telling someone truth is a form of loving that person. It can even be a rather heroic form of love when telling the truth causes you personal embarrassment or gets others angry at you. Again, respecting another's property, protecting the environment, protecting another's reputation, respecting another's body — these are all ways of relating and these are in fact ways of loving the other.

If to be fully human and fully moral is to be in loving relationship with oneself and others, we can guess that sin is the opposite condition. It is failing to love. It is destroying relationships. It is producing alienation. We can see this more clearly in a concrete example.

Danielle is a very attractive and very popular girl. The teachers at her high school like her. Many boys want to date her. She has a large circle of friends. But she has some enemies too, a small clique that is very jealous of her. They begin to spread rumors that she is sleeping around. A few of the boys she has dated keep the rumor going by implying that they have "made it" with her. They lie in order to look "macho" among their buddies.

The bad reputation takes hold even though it's not deserved. Boys try to date Danielle with only one thing in mind. Soon she

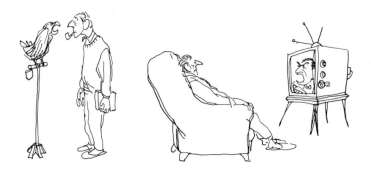

prefers staying at home weekends rather than going through a wrestling match on every date. Within six months she has become almost totally isolated from the school community. She can't shake the reputation no matter how hard she tries. She's depressed, miserable, and lonely . . . That's what sin does.

Or take our example of locked doors. Thieves take things that belong to others. The material loss they cause others is bad enough. But their sin does something much worse than cause some material loss. It causes fear. It forces people to be suspicious of any stranger that passes by. In short, it produces alienation. It destroys human relationships of trust and friendship. In this manner sin affects whole societies.

The victim of someone's sin isn't the only person hurt, though. The sinner is also hurt. A thief, for example, can't afford to trust others either. He or she must live a guarded life to avoid being caught. It becomes impossible to have normal, human relationships with others.

Whenever normal, loving relationships between persons are unnecessarily weakened or destroyed, sin is present in some form. Whether the form is lying, gossip, stealing, bullying, or getting drunk isn't as important as the net result of all sin: it makes it impossible to be in relationship to others. Being human means being in relationship. Sin eats away at our humanness.

The special difficulties teenagers face must be mentioned at

this point. Every teenager has vital tasks to pursue. Two of these are (1) to acquire a healthful sense of identity as a sexual person and (2) to develop new, satisfying relationships based on this maturing identity. In this process some harm to parents and friends is inevitable, caused by our stumbling attempts and honest error. A keynote of any mature relationship, however, is the kind of sensitivity we bring to it with regard to the needs of other persons.

The more completely an act or failure to act destroys relationships, the more serious it is. Too often there is a tendency to focus on the act rather than on the effect it has on relationships. In the above example of the clique, the act was rather trivial — a little gossip. Its effect was deadly, however.

Again, something like vandalism shouldn't be measured only in terms of the amount of damage. It should also be measured in terms of the effect it has on the victim's ability to relate with others. The victim could end up being hateful and distrustful of all youth. This result can't be measured in dollars.

Some acts by their very nature are always seriously sinful. Murder, for example, by its very nature completely destroys the victim's relationships. It cuts a person off from the human race completely. Notice how society has always punished murder. It isolates the murderer from all others — by a life in prison, by exile, or by death itself.

2 Moving into Sin

Doing something that is *mortally* destructive of human relationships takes some doing. It is a radical kind of decision. A person must intend to do it, must be acting freely (not out of fear, coercion, or in an irrational rage), and the person must know just how destructive the action can be. To sin mortally we have to really work at it.

More often people sort of back into a sinful state. A lie here, a lie there, and eventually lying becomes a person's normal way of relating to others. The person has become a liar. A liar has lost the ability to relate to others in a truthful way. We can say the same thing about becoming a thief. Usually a person develops a thieving habit gradually through repeated small acts — cheating on an exam here, taking a few dollars there, slipping out a record under the jacket another time. The pattern develops to the point that the person ceases to have any respect for other people's property. He or she will take anything from anyone anytime a chance occurs. Respect for other people and their property is a part of all human relationships. It's another form of loving. When we have lost it entirely, we are in the state of mortal sinfulness.

So we determine what is serious matter first of all by how important certain qualities are to our humanness. Way back in the first chapter it was suggested that each of us has an inner experience of what the qualities are: love is more human than

hate; respect for our bodies and those of others is more human than abusing our bodies; honesty and truthfulness are more human than lying and deceit; and so forth. To be human means to develop certain kinds of loving relationships with ourselves, with others, and ultimately with God: truthful relationships, respectful relationships, peaceful relationships, helping relationships.

None of us has to be a moral theologian to have a basic awareness of what is the more human and the less human relationship. More often than not, no one has to tell us when we've developed to a point where we have lost one of these essential forms of loving. We know it from within, and we live with it every day.

In the same way no one has to tell us when a single act of ours is so serious by its nature or its consequences that by that single act we've freely, knowingly, deliberately destroyed some relationship with others. So while theologians may have a complicated concept of what a sin — and particularly a mortal sin — is, our own common sense and our own inner experience of ourselves is often sufficient to tell us when we've become sinful.

This is not to say that we can't sometimes be the victims of our own ignorance or of misinformation. In regard to pre-marital sex, for instance, the questions which crop up in discussions reflect our ignorance: "Who will it hurt?" often paired up with "Why not? It's fun!" The fact is, as people with experience in sexual matters can testify, sex isn't always fun, indeed sex can hurt people, and as

many lives have been harmed by sex which turned out to be some kind of insult or disillusionment as have been healed and made joyful by it.

Moreover, on top of our honest ignorance about sexual matters, we are exposed to gross misinformation by popular media. The constant message we are fed in show after show, in song after song sounds like a silly song lyric itself: "Bedding down with anyone is better than bedding down with no one at all. And the only sin — besides pimples — is being alone."

As another example of misinformation, many moral people find that they can support abortion-on-demand because scientific and legal authorities have misled them to believe that killing a fetus is not killing a person or not killing at all.

So people can do inhuman things not knowing any better and experience no sense of sinfulness. Nor does the habit-forming result of continually making wrong decisions apply here. We don't expect a driver who accidentally killed someone with a car to become a career murderer, for example. In fact, such events usually prompt our sympathy because when the dawn of understanding arrives for people in these situations, the results can be the stuff Greek tragedies are made of. An example of this kind of enlightenment is the experience of Bernard N. Nathan, M.D., who was an early supporter of legalized abortion. Dr. Nathan later resigned from his post with an abortion clinic, explaining

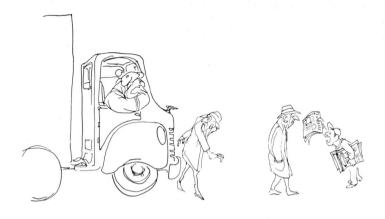

that he had become uneasy over the fact that he "had in fact presided over 60,000 deaths."

3 Sin and God

Now let's try to make some sense out of the idea that something like missing Mass could be labeled a mortal sin. It is important to remember that being Christian implies having certain kinds of relationships with God too. We owe God many of the same things we owe other persons: respect for his person and name, respect for the creation he has made available to us — which includes our own person. Further, we owe God something precisely because he is God, namely our worship, our willingness to admit that he is God and we are his creatures. Refusing to worship God, presuming we have arrived at a conscious belief in his existence, is to destroy a quality fundamental to our relationship as a human person with God.

It is safe to say, then, that if you believe in God and your relationship with him, whatever you deliberately do to destroy that relationship is sinful. What about the Church? It is a visible community with an institutional, public, or tangible dimension. People belong to it by free choice. These people share a common faith and a common understanding of what it means to be fully human — a moral code. This community believes, among other

things, that our relationship to God means to worship God not just privately but publicly as a community on a regular basis.

To consciously, deliberately, and continually refuse to participate in this communal worship is considered serious enough that such persons are considered to have put themselves outside the Church. They have destroyed one of their fundamental human relationships with God: communal worship. Thus to miss Mass continually with the conscious intention of severing that relationship with God is considered a mortal sin by the Church.

While missing Mass is serious in itself from the Church's point of view, the occasional absentee is seldom committing what could be called a mortal sin — a final break with all communal worship in keeping with the Church's tradition. He or she might be guilty of laziness, apathy, insensitivity to the needs and feelings of others, but not rejection of God. As with all such serious acts, we are more interested in the pattern that develops, the real motives behind the absenteeism, what is happening to the person.

This understanding about why the breaking of certain Church laws was labeled a mortal sin got lost in a legalistic mentality at one point in the Church. The law became more important than what the law was trying to teach us about our humanness and our relationship to God and neighbor. The legalism generated that kind of moral minimum we talked about earlier. Instead of asking how we might become more fully human and using the law as a guide, people asked how far they could bend a law without break-

Silverstein

ing it. Hopefully that is past history, even though a few traces of it still remain within the Church community.

Once a person has chosen not to develop essential relationships, especially by a long series of repeated choices, the road back is not easy. If getting into the state of mortal sinfulness takes radical decisions, getting back out takes the same kind of decisions. To take hold of one's life again, to give it a radical new direction, to cease following a pattern that has built up over a long period is not easy, but it is possible.

Typically, this process is called conversion. Unlike the popular notion, conversions are seldom instantaneous. They build up over a period of time. The prodigal son in the gospel is a good example. He didn't give up his swinging lifestyle easily. He hung on until the last dollar was spent. Even then, it took him some time associating with pigs before he finally figured out his life was a mess and the only thing to do was go back home and start over. His conversion is probably more typical than was Paul's on the road to Damascus.

That's why it makes more sense to check out one's moral patterns of behavior continually. One fight isn't bad, but getting into fights every weekend should begin to tell us something. We are losing our respect for the life and health of ourselves and others. It's time to quit before this necessary respect is gone altogether.

4 Sin and Community

This is another dimension to sin which we haven't mentioned yet. We have seen, from a common sense point of view, how our weaker moral choices can in fact develop habits which destroy our ability to love. But we are involved in more than what psychologists ordinarily can cure by counseling or therapy. When we speak of sin we enter the realm of evil, a spiritual reality that follows its own laws, many of which we don't fully understand.

A thoroughly corrupted person, an extreme case of the power of evil, often seeks "converts" with much the same zeal as a missionary. Moreover, a person in the state of sin will often draw others into sin by persuasion, enticement, trickery, promises of the "good life." Charles Manson's tactics, made so public by the motion picture *Helter Skelter,* come to mind. Drug pushers are known to give their junk to young children — to the point where the kids become hooked and dependent on the pusher. Kiddie pornography is perhaps the most vicious example of how someone who has lost all respect for the human person seeks to spread that infection to innocent children.

In fact it is impossible to completely escape the influence of evil at work in any society. It is all around us. This doesn't mean we are totally free of guilt if we become entrapped by some form of sinfulness. To be sinful means to have chosen to be sinful. But to be Christian doesn't mean being sinless either; it means choosing to be a loving human like Jesus.

So it is never just a question of sin being a personal matter, or something between you and God. Because of the very nature of sin, its effects are always a social matter, a community matter. We all are affected by the sinfulness of one of us. As Christians we strive to build an environment which promotes moral health rather than sickness, one in which people can grow to be fully human.

Another important point follows from this. We can talk of communal sin. A whole group can cooperate in sinfulness. The danger with this kind of communal sinfulness, whether it takes place on a high school campus or throughout a whole nation, is that no one individual necessarily feels responsible. Typical reactions are "What did *I* do?" or "What could *I* do?" There is a kind of deceiving anonymity or facelessness when we deal with communal sinfulness. Whom do you blame when a whole corporation plots to defraud its customers? How do you get a whole class of students to feel responsible for what happens to one person in their midst? How does a whole group "convert" from its sinfulness?

So morality is more than a personal self-improvement program. The personal moral decisions we make always have an effect on the various groups we belong to. They either make it a more sinful or a more morally wholesome situation for everybody. The personal moral choices of others — especially those with whom you associate most closely — have the same kind of effect on you. They affect the moral environment in which you must strive to become fully human.

5 Sin and Grace

There is one final fact about the evil involved in sinfulness. Sin has an enslaving power. It can make us morally blind and make us feel virtually helpless to recover moral health unaided. Yet we've said that anyone can recover moral wholeness up to the point of physical death. There is always hope.

This doesn't mean we can always recover totally on our own power. Changing from a sinful state to one of moral integrity requires outside help. We need to be touched by a goodness that is more powerful than our sinfulness. We need to experience a love that is stronger than our hate, a self*less*ness that is stronger than our self*ish*ness.

From the point of view of faith we call this grace: God's intervention in our lives to rescue us, to free us from the trap we are in. This intervention doesn't come in miraculous ways. It usually takes place within very natural events — and often even has a negative look to it.

Almost dying from an overdose, for instance, is often enough to get a drug user to seek a cure and get his/her life straightened out. Almost getting caught in a burglary is often enough to convince someone that it's time to get out of the stealing thing. A girl who discovers that she's getting a reputation for being a pushover might decide her present sexual lifestyle is ruining her chances for the good marriage she actually desires. Getting cut up in a fight might help a person decide the tough-guy routine isn't the way to go. It is in just these kinds of circumstances that healthful guilt — accepting the harm we have done and feeling sorrow over it — can begin to heal us and help us to change.

But this grace that jars one from a sinful lifestyle and enables a person — almost propels a person — into a conversion to a morally wholesome life doesn't always have to come from bad experiences or near misses. Just as often it can come from good experiences, including directly religious ones. For instance, a group might go to a Billy Graham type rally "just for kicks" with no serious intentions; yet, somehow the message gets to them, and they end up taking a serious look at where their present lifestyle is taking them.

A good friend who is also a good person can turn our life around, bring us to our senses, encourage us to change. Not so much by preaching or nagging, but by love, support, concern, and good example. It is not rare for someone to become a moral person because he/she has met and fallen in love with some loving and vital person.

There's one thing to remember in all this. Precisely because we often need this outside help, this grace, to free ourselves from the power of evil, we need to know that help is always available. God is always offering us grace. Even reading this book could be such an offering. Scripture tells that sin is strong, but that God's love is stronger. Even though evil surrounds us, God's help is always present and active. It's just a question of looking around and of accepting help in whatever form it comes.

6 Sin and Reconciliation

Once a person has experienced such a change from a state of sinfulness to that of seeking to be morally whole again, one more step is usually necessary — going public. In recent times we've seen some rather highly publicized "conversions." There is the case of one of the more notorious of the Watergate criminals. Without disclosing the details of how he gained grace, he declares that he has become convinced of the evil of his past life and is seeking to dedicate himself to more noble causes now. On the one hand, what he experienced was a private matter. It took place within himself. Yet he felt a need to go public, to admit to everyone how wrong he had been and to publicly promise he would do better. Though some may regard this as a cheap publicity stunt, there is sound psychology working here.

Our conversion from a sinful state really isn't complete, isn't put on solid ground, until we go public. We mentioned that all sinfulness has a social dimension. Likewise recovery from sinfulness needs a social dimension. There is an inner drive at work here. The "confession" is more a celebration than anything else. It celebrates, aims at telling the world, how great it feels to be freed from whatever it was that enslaved us. And this celebration has the effect of making our conversion even more solid and gives us a real impetus and reinforcement to pursue a more morally wholesome lifestyle.

It is in this context that we can better appreciate what the Church is trying to do through the Sacrament of Reconciliation. This sacrament is a public celebration of what has already begun in private.

We experience a grace which convinces us to reject some sinful lifestyle. In approaching the Sacrament of Reconciliation two things take place. We go public, admit to the sinfulness, and reject it. More importantly, we are also celebrating the cure, rejoicing in how God has reached in and helped us get straightened out. The very celebration has the effect of strengthening our determination to stay straightened out.

In the Sacrament of Reconciliation, though, going public doesn't mean we stand up in front of the whole community and shout out all our past sinful acts in all their gory details. Just approaching the sacrament is all the declaration one needs to the community at large. Even in talking to the priest who represents the community, it is enough to state that one has become a thief, or a seducer, or a destroyer of people's reputations. We don't have to, nor are we expected to, go into all the details, many of which can be painful to recall and usually very embarrassing to relate. In other words we aren't expected to go in with a list explaining the stains on our dirty laundry. It is enough to say we need a new shirt or socks or pair of pants because we've ruined the old ones. This is all done in the context of a celebration of the fact that God has already intervened, that we have already found the courage to reject a former lifestyle. So the emphasis is much more on what God is doing for us than on whatever it was we had done to ourselves and others.

To put all this another way, we approach the sacrament to celebrate a conversion, not to experience one. The conversion one brings to the sacrament is then ratified, strengthened, confirmed, made "official." Even one's willingness to approach the sacrament is proof that the conversion has already begun. People who are still comfortable with and have no plans to change their sinful lifestyle — or haven't become convinced that it is a sinful lifestyle — simply don't approach the sacrament. They just won't see any value or use for it. At least not yet.

The Sacrament of Reconciliation isn't reserved just for those who had become entrapped by some form of mortal sinfulness, though it is especially intended for them. In fact, probably most people who approach the sacrament aren't involved in mortal sinfulness. They come because they have begun to notice patterns developing that could lead to such a state of mortal sinfulness. It is these patterns of selfishness, of lying, of disrespect for other people's person or property that they seek to reject and turn from.

The goal is to root out all sinfulness from our lives, not just its extreme or deadly forms. That's why any person motivated by faith in the Christian moral vision will recognize the Sacrament of Reconciliation as valuable in a regular or on-going way, not just in those extreme — and possibly rare — instances where we are involved in mortal sinfulness.

Sin, then, and the mystery of evil in which it lives, is more than a few hang-ups or bad habits or character defects. It has the power to destroy human relationships. It can be countered only by a power greater than itself — the powerful, forgiving, recreative love of God, shown to us in events and in others.

7 Thinking It Over: Sin

A. Define what you consider to be the nature of sin.

Describe what *you* consider to be the necessary qualities an act must have to be judged a mortally sinful act, based upon your definition of sin.

Do you think that kind of mortally sinful action is common or rare in the lives of most people? Why or why not? Be prepared to share and discuss your own answers with others in the class.

B. List as many actions you can think of that are considered to be sinful in most circumstances by the Church and/or by your parent(s) that you personally don't consider to be sinful or wrong in most circumstances.

1) _____   3) _____

2) _____   4) _____

5) _____   8) _____

6) _____   9) _____

7) _____   10) _____

Be prepared to discuss why you disagree with the position of the Church and/or your parent(s).

C. Think of and list any movies, TV stories, novels, or real life instances where a person or group had been involved in a sinful lifestyle but experienced a conversion to a morally good lifestyle — for example, Johnny Cash's life story.

1) _____   4) _____

2) _____   5) _____

3) _____   6) _____

What event(s) or person(s) would you consider to be the "grace" in the examples you've come up with?

Share your examples and the "graces" you've identified with others in the class.

In the light of this discussion spend a few minutes reflecting privately on any "grace" you have experienced in the last year: something that jarred you out of a sinful direction.

Are there any "graces" at work in your life right now? From what are they calling you? *You are not expected to share these reflections with others.*

CHAPTER 7

Advice and Authority:
Whom Should We Listen To?

There is one final dimension to explore in terms of your moral development: you are not alone. It's true that you are ultimately responsible for your own moral decisions. This doesn't mean, though, that you are expected to work out everything all by yourself.

In fact, it is often much better to work many things through with others, to seek advice of more experienced persons. This includes parents. Most parents are very concerned about the happiness and welfare of their children. Chances are your parents are included in that group. They may not be moral giants, and they probably have a few faults of their own. But they do have two things going for them: they want what is best for you, and they've been around long enough to have learned a few things the hard way.

Unfortunately parents often express their concern in negative ways. "No, you can't go to that party." "I don't want you hanging around with those kids." "I don't care if everyone else is going. You aren't and that's final."

Youth typically feel their parents are being unreasonable, and therefore there is no sense trying to talk with them. Communications break off on all but the most superficial level.

Hopefully, you won't fall into that trap. If you can get behind what sounds like a negative attitude, you'll see what is really motivating them. You'll discover it's love — and some reasonable fears. Check out your own thinking. Are you fooling yourself? Why do you think something is good and your parents don't? Above all keep the lines of communication open. Getting all worked up and emotional usually just makes things worse. Taking time to talk through your own position with them and taking time to really listen to your parents' reasoning is critical. Even if you still can't agree with them, you'll at least learn there is more than one way to look at many moral issues. Also they will see more clearly by your very desire to dialogue with them (dialogue, not argue) that you are taking your own moral development seriously. You are searching. You truly want to do what's right. Parents need to see that. Too often we don't take the time to show them. That's why they feel they must still treat us like little children. Much the same thing can be said for other important adults in your life. Most of these people are eager to assist you as you work through your moral decisions.

Remember, being human means being in relationship. One very real form of loving relationship is your willingness to seek advice from others. Some people hesitate to seek advice because they feel their concerns are so unique that maybe something is wrong with them. Others hesitate because they fear the adults will force their own opinions onto them.

While these fears can be experienced as very real, they are almost always rooted in unreality. Not having all the answers worked out yet is very normal. No one can force their opinions on you. Again, you and only you can make your own moral decisions. Seeking advice doesn't mean you must automatically follow it.

1 The Light of Experience

There is one other place where you can seek help in forming your own moral life: it is the Church, which includes — besides your parents — teachers, priests, and school counselors or youth ministers. There's a problem here, though.

Let us suppose that, having come out of a Christian childhood, you are basically comfortable with Jesus' explanation (and demonstration) of what it means to be fully human — that fundamentally you have a Christian conscience. Your own experience supports it. Generosity and concern for others is better than selfishness. Forgiving your enemy is more human than seeking vengeance. The goods of this world are gifts to be shared, not prizes to be won. All of humankind are intended to live in peace and harmony; no person or group should be excluded from our concern.

These are tough ideals to live up to and you fail once in a while, but in the long run these kinds of ideals shape your own moral decisions. So far so good. The problem for most of us comes when we introduce the notion of the Church and morality. What right does the Church have to determine that this or that particular action contradicts what Jesus taught us about being human? Jesus didn't get all that specific on a lot of things. Where does he say, for example, that masturbation is wrong? or contraception? or getting high once in a while? or refusing to go to Sunday Mass?

In the last analysis if each of us is alone in making moral decisions and each of us possesses a freedom here that no person or institution can violate, how can anyone say we are obligated to follow the Church's teaching on moral questions and to form our conscience around that teaching?

First, there is a certain legitimacy to these kinds of objections. For one thing, even the Church admits that it has no right to force, trick, or manipulate anyone to contradict his or her own conscience on any concrete moral decision. Second, it is true that the gospel and its companion, the Hebrew Scriptures, do not give us a book of answers for every moral decision that we face. For example, Jesus didn't give us one direct idea about what our stance should be regarding the morality of organ transplants or of genetic engineering to pre-determine the sex of a human embryo. The Church really can't base all of its moral teaching directly on what Jesus said and did.

The real issue, then, is what we mean by Church and how the Church arrives at its moral teachings not directly found in the words and actions of Jesus. For too many people the "teaching" Church continues to have a very narrow meaning: a nameless, faceless group of aging bishops over in Rome sitting around issuing laws about how everybody else must live. In fact, the Church is a living, dynamic community struggling to apply Jesus' general teaching to the kinds of specific decisions it must make. It's a community that has been doing this for almost two thousand years.

For example, the early Church wasn't clear on a lot of things. It had to operate out of its own experience. There was not universal agreement on a lot of things at first. It was a kind of trial and error — with aid from the Spirit. For example, could a Christian be true to Christ and go to the Roman Games? Could a Christian be true to Christ and own slaves — a legal right of that time? Could a Christian be true to Christ and serve in the army?

Decisions about these kinds of moral problems evolved slowly. Eventually the Christian community came to the conclusion that the Games contradicted the *spirit* of what Jesus taught. Eventually Christians came to the conclusion that they should free their slaves. It was the more Christ-like and therefore the more human thing to do.

This kind of evolution is the source of all the Church's moral teaching on matters not directly taught by Jesus or found in scripture. It was the interaction of the community's lived experience seeking out the spirit of what Jesus taught with a certain amount of trial and error. These evolving conclusions eventually came to be considered official teaching. The pope and bishops were in charge of handing the official teachings to the next generation.

Each new generation had to evaluate the teachings arrived at in the past in the light of its own experience. Many of these teachings stood the test of time. They remained true. Others were changed or even dropped entirely as new insights and new experiences expanded the community's understanding. For example, the Christian community in the Middle Ages saw nothing wrong with crusades or holy wars to free the Holy Land from the "infidel." Later the Christian community couldn't justify itself doing something similar — even if it had military power at its disposal. What the Christian community judged morally okay in one time in history, with its unique circumstances and with its particular kind of limited knowledge, was judged morally wrong later both because circumstances were different and because the Christian community had matured over the centuries.

2 Issues in the Church Today

That's the situation today. This same Christian community living in the last half of the twentieth century must evaluate the teachings of the past in the light of its own experience and circumstances. Many of the interpretations of what Jesus taught remain valid for us today. Some are being rejected in light of new understanding and new experience. Like our ancestors before us we must also struggle with problems that have never been faced by the Christian community before.

For example, when it comes to things like organ transplants or "pulling the plug" on people being kept alive by totally artificial means, today's Church has no tradition to fall back upon or even alter. Jesus taught us to respect our bodies and to respect all life. What that means in these concrete circumstances with our new medical skill we really don't know yet. We are to a large degree in the trial-and-error stage of developing an explicit teaching on those topics.

Probably one of the most publicized and controversial moral teachings of the Christian community today revolves around the question of birth control by artificial means. Our past tradition bans it outright as contrary to what Jesus implicitly taught us about the nature and purpose of marriage and sexual intercourse. However, this tradition contradicts the experience of many Chris-

tians today. Also we face new circumstances never faced before, like overpopulation and the fact that many poor countries with large Christian populations face real danger of starvation if the birth rate is not reduced. Also we have arrived at a broadened understanding of the marriage relationship which includes more than just making babies. The mutual spiritual growth of the husband and wife is also a legitimate end for marriage.

Why, then, doesn't the official Church change its traditional position in the light of what the overall Christian community is experiencing? For one thing, the Church is always very careful about overthrowing official teaching. It is operating out of almost two thousand years of experience and has too often seen that a "majority" view even within the Church is no automatic proof that the view is the true interpretation of Jesus' teaching.

Second, on such an important matter with potential conse-

quences for the rest of human history, a swift reversal could be seen as irresponsible, giving in to pressure just to keep the membership high — and the collections profitable.

Given time for the entire Christian community to reflect on just what is an accurate interpretation of Jesus' teaching about being human, loving, giving, and serving, the official Church may in fact alter its traditional teaching eventually. In any case, each person in a couple must ultimately confront such decisions alone. It is repeated in several Vatican II documents, as a teaching of the Church, that every person is bound to follow his or her conscience "in order that he may come to God." Following the decision-making procedure presented in this book, it is necessary in such important decisions (1) to get the facts, (2) to seek advice, and (3) to reflect on Jesus' teachings in thought and in prayer. The facts in this case include a real understanding of the Church's teaching as well as a sensitivity to particular circumstances — size of family, financial condition, health, and more.

In this case, the person must take the time to both know and understand why the official Church is saying what it is saying. Many times an individual rejects a moral teaching of the Church without really knowing what it says and why. To have a Christian conscience we are expected to form our own personal conscience *in the light of* the tradition of our ancestors. We must have solid reasons to reject a particular part of it and to form our consciences contrary to it. And we had better be in touch with our motives in the process.

Does any of this have any real application to you? It does if you consider the life and teaching of Jesus to be the best overall explanation of what it really means to be human. You have at your disposal the experience of two thousand years of other Christians who faced the same struggle to apply Jesus' teaching to the concrete problems not specifically mentioned by Jesus. No soldier arriving at the front lines for the first time rejects offhand the advice of the veteran who has been there six months. If the veteran survived that long, he must be doing something right.

The same kind of thing is true for ourselves in relation to our Christian ancestors. They must have learned something about what it means to be authentically human, or that faith in Jesus would have died out long ago.

But just as the new recruit might have to work out some things for himself because the enemy now has new weapons, so we are expected to work out some moral decisions never faced by our ancestors.

It would be foolish to totally ignore the advice of the veteran soldier. It would be irresponsible also to blindly follow all the advice without making any effort to adapt it to new situations.

The same is obviously true for the Christian. To totally ignore all the moral advice of a two thousand year tradition would be rather foolish. To follow every word of it slavishly without seeking to enrich and adapt it to this present time would be immature if not irresponsible.

If push comes to shove, it can be observed that about 95 percent of the official moral teaching the Church has developed over the centuries is basically common sense application of the kind of inner moral code we all experience within us. Very little of it at any one point in history can be considered controversial or as going against the grain of the shared experience of the majority of the Christian community. In our day most of the real controversy revolves, as we said, around moral questions related to marriage, like birth control and divorce.

The rest of the controversy within the Church is related to theological matters like ordination of women, bishops' and pastors' powers in relation to the laity, and to questions regarding the meaning of original sin or the evolutionary origin of humanity. These kinds of controversies are important for the Church, but in terms of the day-to-day moral decisions we face they really don't apply. They do have a moral dimension such as the potential injustice being done to women in the Church but to resolve them won't really help us decide things like the morality of planned parenthood or of living together to decide if a marriage would work.

Finally we can observe that actually the majority of the Church's moral tradition is not expressed in official teachings about the *minimum* we must or must not do to be human. Rather it is a tradition of spiritual advice about how to become a more loving, selfless, fully human person. It is an application of the moral teaching of Jesus contained in things like the Sermon on the Mount.

So becoming morally mature need not be something you work out alone. Parents and other adults have a lot to share with you. The Church has centuries of experience to share with you. Finally, God is on your side too, and praying over tough moral decisions is often a great help.

We've come to an end. There is much more we could get into. The goal has been to help you think through your own understanding of what it means to be human, what it means to be moral, what is involved in making moral decisions, and what the results are after you've made those decisions.

Once you get all that straightened out for yourself — using whatever help this book or any other source can provide — you'll be in a good position to think through these problems yourself and also to evaluate the solutions offered by those who are operating out of a Christian moral vision.

Probably — hopefully — you are rather near the point of getting it together. Hang in there. It is worth the effort.

3 Thinking It Over: Advice and Authority

A. *Looking Behind the Rules*

Your parent(s) probably still enforces certain rules on you, for instance, when you have to get home on weekends, evenings, particulars about using the family car, and the like.

Below list any of those rules with which you personally disagree. Then try to identify the probable reason, value, or need of your parent(s) that underlies the rule. Finally, identify your own reason, value, or need that causes you to disagree with the rule.

1) Rule: _____

    Parents' reason for the rule: _____

    _____

    Your reason for disagreeing with rule: _____

    _____

2) Rule: _____

    Parents' reason for the rule: _____

    _____

    Your reason for disagreeing with rule: _____

    _____

3) Rule: _____

    Parents' reason for the rule: _____

    _____

    Your reason for disagreeing with rule: _____

    _____

You may now want to share your results with others in the class to see if you have similar problems, patterns of thinking, and the like.

Finally, you may want to share the results with your parent(s). Do you honestly know what is behind the rule, from their point of view? Do they really know why you disagree with the rule? Would it be possible to work out some kind of compromise in which both your parents' needs and your own needs are satisfied?

B. *Where to Go for Help*

Here is a list of possible people you could go to in order to work out a decision involving your morality and your conscience. You can add others:

older brother or sister
parents
aunt, uncle
close friend in your class
priest
Religious Sister or Brother
teacher
school counselor
coach
books on the topic
advice column in paper
Sacrament of Reconciliation

Here are three situations. Under each list your first, second, and third choice of whom you would be willing to talk with to get advice. If you would talk to no one, give your reason.

1) You have a chance to get the answers to a very important test ahead of time. Cheating like that bothers you, but if you fail the test it could affect your chance at getting into a college.

With whom would you possibly talk before you make your decision?

a) _____

b) _____

c) _____

If no one, why?

2) Your sixteen-year-old sister is pregnant. She confides in you and asks you to help her get an abortion before your parents find out. You really want to help her, but you're not sure abortion is the answer. In fact you are convinced it's seriously immoral.

With whom would you possibly talk in order to decide what you should do for your sister?

a) _____

b) _____

c) _____

If no one, why?

3) You are going steady and plan to get married as soon as possible. Because of the seriousness of your relationship, your steady is not opposed to pre-marital sex. You find yourself leaning in that direction too, but your conscience still tells you it's sinful.

With whom would you possibly talk to get advice:

a) _____

b) _____

c) _____

If no one, why?

Now, compare with others in the class the kinds of people you would probably rely on to get the best moral advice.

If you really doubt that you would seek advice from others except in the most extreme kind of case, discuss why you feel that way.

C. *New Problems*

We have said that today the Church faces moral questions that it never had to face before. Jesus never talked directly about any of these questions. The Church must try to decide in the light of the spirit behind the teaching of Jesus. You are part of that Church.

In small groups, discuss and try to decide the moral goodness or badness of each of the following. Be prepared to share your decisions with the other groups in the class. Be prepared to give your reasons for the decisions.

Problem One: Test-tube babies.

Problem Two: Cloning.

Problem Three: Removing life support systems from someone who is in a permanent coma due to brain damage.

Problem Four: Genetic engineering to predetermine the sex of a fetus.

Problem Five: The homosexual's rights within the Church.

ACKNOWLEDGMENTS
Webb Photos, cover; John Arms, page 2; Norman Provost, FSC, pages 6, 36, 50; Jean-Claude LeJeune, pages 14, 78; Rohn Engh, page 18; *The Co-Worker Newsletter*, page 76; Shel Silverstein, pages 80-90, from *The Classic Cartoons*, edited by William Cole and Mike Thaler, World Publishing Company, reproduced by special permission of Playboy Magazine, copyright 1960 by Playboy; NC News Service, page 98; Daniel D. Miller, pages 104-105.